THE
ABCs
OF Gold
Investing

How to Protect and Build Your Wealth With Gold

SECOND EDITION

Michael J. Kosares

Addicus Books
Omaha, Nebraska

An Addicus Nonfiction Book

ISBN# 1-886039-72-0
Cover design by George Foster
Graphs and charts by Topline Investment Graphics

Library of Congress Cataloging-in-Publication Data

Kosares, Michael J., 1948-
   The ABCs of gold investing : how to protect and build your wealth with gold / Michael J. Kosares.— 2nd ed.
     p. cm.
"An Addicus Nonfiction Book."
Includes bibliographical references and index.
ISBN 1-886039-72-0 (alk. Paper)
   1. Gold—Purchasing—United States. 2. Investments—United States. I. Title.
   HG295.U6K67 2004
   332.63—dc2   2004016618

Addicus Books, Inc.
P.O. Box 45327
Omaha, Nebraska 68145
Web site: www.AddicusBooks.com

Printed in the United States of America
10 9 8 7 6 5 4 3 2

To the golden fraternity, the owners, advocates, pundits, and professionals who have kept the flame alive.

Contents

Acknowledgments

The following organizations played an instrumental role in bringing this book to fruition: Gold Fields Mineral Services, Ltd. of London, England, U.K.; the World Gold Council of New York; the Gold Institute; the United States Mint; the Austrian Mint; the Royal Canadian Mint; the Gold Corporation of Australia; the South African Chamber of Mines; the American Numismatic Association; the Mexican Consulate in Denver, Colorado, U.S.A.; the Industry Council for Tangible Assets; and TopLine Investment Graphics of Colorado.

For their prompt and complete support, I owe these organizations a huge debt of gratitude. Last but not least, I would like to thank Dr. Henry Swenson, who gave me the idea for this book in the first place. Without them, *The ABCs of Gold Investing* would have remained an unrealized dream.

Introduction

This book is a distillation of over thirty years' experience working with private investors interested in adding gold to their investment portfolios. For many years, investors looking for a "how to" guide on private gold ownership have come home from the bookstore empty-handed. With the publication of this guideline, a basic who, what, when, where, why, and how of private gold ownership is now available.

Over the past decade, the primary motivation for gold ownership has been asset preservation as stock markets around the world went into a tailspin, yields trended toward zero, and the dollar suddenly fell from grace on international markets. Gold performed that safe-haven function in admirable fashion. Now a new motivation for gold ownership has entered the market, one rooted in a dynamic shift in gold's supply–demand fundamentals, and strongly suggesting the possibility of much higher prices in the months and years to come. In addition to gold's bedrock role in the financial portfolio as the ultimate fiduciary asset, many investors have now begun to view gold as an architect of wealth. Almost on cue, the long dormant price has begun to rise in international markets with the metal logging price increases of over 20 percent in both 2002 and 2003. Many market experts see this as the opening salvo ushering in a new secular bull market in gold—one in which emerging market fundamentals, combined with concerns about the overall economy and financial markets, could potentially drive gold prices to levels we have not seen since the late 1970s.

With investor sentiment shifting in gold's direction, this book could not have come at a better time. You now have in your hands a practical and comprehensive "how to" manual for making an informed decision about gold ownership. Perhaps gold can offer you what it has offered countless others over the centuries: solid unassailable protection against the gathering storm as well as a means to building your personal wealth despite uncertain times.

Michael J. Kosares
Denver, Colorado

*Indeed, there can be no other criterion, no other standard
than gold. Yes, gold which never changes, which can be
shaped into ingots, bars, coins, which has no nationality
and which is eternally and universally accepted as the
unalterable fiduciary value par excellence.*
—Charles DeGaulle

1

A is for ...
Asset Preservation:
Why Americans Need Gold

> *The possession of gold has ruined fewer men
> than the lack of it.*
> —Thomas Bailey Aldrich

The incident is one of the most memorable of my career.
Never before or since has the value of gold in preserving
assets been made so abundantly clear to me. It was the
mid-1970s. The United States was finally extricating itself from
the conflict in South Vietnam. Thousands of South Vietnamese had fled their embattled homeland rather than face the
vengeance of the rapidly advancing Communist forces.

In my Denver office, a couple from South Vietnam who
had been part of that exodus sat across from me. They had
come to sell their gold. In broken English, the man told me
the story of how he and his wife had escaped the fall of Saigon and certain reprisal by North Vietnamese troops. They
got out with nothing more than a few personal belongings
and the small cache of gold he now spread before me on my
desk. His eyes widened as he explained why they were lucky
to have survived those last fearful days of the South Vietnamese Republic. They had scrambled onto a fishing boat and

had sailed into the South China Sea, where they were rescued by the U.S. Navy. These were Vietnamese "boat people," survivors of that chapter in the tragedy of Indochina. Now they were about to redeem their life savings in gold so that they could start a new business in the United States.

Their gold wrapped in rice paper was a type called *Kim Thanh*. These are the commonly traded units in Hong Kong and throughout the Far East. Kim Thanh weigh about 1.2 troy ounces, or a *tael*, as it is called in the Orient. They look like thick gold leaf rectangles 3 to 4 inches long, 1-1/2 to 2 inches wide, and a few millimeters deep. Kim Thanh are embossed with Oriental characters describing weight and purity. As a gesture to the Occident, they are stamped in the center with the words OR PUR, "pure gold."

It wasn't much gold—about 30 ounces—but it might as well have been a ton. The couple considered themselves very fortunate to have escaped with this small hoard of gold. They thanked me profusely for buying it. As we talked about Vietnam and their future in the United States, I couldn't help but become caught up in their enthusiasm for the future. These resilient, hard-working, thrifty people now had a new lease on life. When they left my office that day, there was little doubt in my mind that they would be successful in their new life. It was rewarding to know that gold could do this for them. It was satisfying to know that I had helped them in this small way.

I kept those golden Kim Thanh for many years. They became something of a symbol for me—a reminder of the power and importance of gold. Today, when economic and financial problems have begun to signal deeper, more fundamental concerns for the United States, I still remember that Vietnamese couple and how important gold can be to a family's future. Had the couple escaped with South Vietnamese paper money instead of gold, I could have done nothing for them. There was no exchange rate for the South Vietnamese currency because there was no longer a South Vietnam! Wisely, they had converted their savings to gold long before the helicopters lifted U.S. diplomats off the roof of the American Embassy in 1975.

Over the years, I have come to understand and appreciate the many important uses of gold—artistic, cultural, economic, and industrial. Gold is unsurpassed for jewelry and as a high-tech conductor of electricity. Gold has medical applications in dentistry and in treating diseases from arthritis to cancer. Gold plating is used in computers and in many other information-age technologies. All of these pale, though, in light of gold's ancient function as money. As an asset of last resort, gold makes its most important contribution to the general welfare. Through the many economic debacles in human history runs one common thread: those who survive financially do so because they own gold. In recent years, gold has regained its glitter among American investors. This renewed interest in gold is not so much a hedge against the devastation of war but against something much more subtle—the potential destruction of wealth from an international collapse of the dollar and a subsequent economic breakdown.

The Stressed U.S. Economy

The telltale symptoms of a currency and an economy in stress dominate the U.S. financial and political scene. The litany is familiar: massive federal government deficits, a burdensome and virtually unpayable national debt, a rapidly growing foreign-held debt, unsustainable levels of private indebtedness, confiscatory taxation, high structural inflation rates, and declining productivity across the board. However, only a handful understand that these problems are interrelated and deeply rooted, and that they directly affect the viability and value of investment portfolios for all Americans. These problems have not suddenly appeared on the horizon, demanding attention. They have been with us for a long time, and they have been steadily eating away at the foundation of the American economy: the value of the U.S. dollar. Many are hoping this deteriorating situation will simply disappear, but

Figure 1. Disturbing Trends

Item	1970	2004	Change
Population	205 million	290 million	+ 41.5%
Median Income	$9,867.00	$42,400	+ 429.0%
Fed Expenditures	$198.6	$2300.0 (est.)	+ 1158.1%
Fed Interest Paid (annual)	$16.2	$156.8	+ 967.9%
Accumulated Fed Debt	$380.9	$6,997.9	+ 1837.2%
Budget Deficit (annual)	$14.4	$477.0 (2004 est.)	+ 3312.5%
Fed Debt Held by Foreigners	$12.4	$1,708.00 (9-31-03)	+ 1377.4%
Trade Deficit	Balanced	$490.0 (2004 est.)	
Consumer Price Index	37.8	185.8	+ 491.5%
Money Supply (M3)	$618.3	$8,862.48	+ 1433.3%
Purchasing Power of Dollar	$1	$.21	- 79.0%
Dow Jones Industrial Average	744.10	10,453.92	+ 1404.9%
Gold	$36.02 (avg.)	$416.25	+ 1155.6%

Monetary figures in Billions

Sources: Department of Commerce, Department of the Treasury and Hussman Econometrics

most of us know that is unlikely. More likely, the situation will worsen.

Just as our bodies adjust to and become inured to the cold, so too our minds have become dulled by the repetitive, steady drumbeat of statistics that prove our economy is in crisis (Figure 1).

In 1970, the budget deficit was a meager $2.8 billion. By December 2003, it had reached $477 billion—170 times the 1970 figure.

- In 1970, the accumulated federal debt was $436 billion. By December 2003, it threatened the $7 trillion mark. This figure does not include so-called off-budget items like long-term Social Security and Medicare obligations, which balloon that figure by multiples.

- Exports and imports were roughly balanced in 1970. The last time the United States ran a trade surplus was 1975. By 2003 year's end, the trade deficit was estimated to be a dismal $490 billion for the year.

- In the process, the United States has gone from being the greatest creditor nation on earth to being the world's greatest debtor nation. In 1970, U.S. debt held by foreigners was a mere $12.4 million. By the end of 2003, it approached a dizzying $1.5 trillion. The problem of foreign-held debt has become so acute that some experts wonder whether the United States will be capable of pursuing its own monetary policy in the future, or whether the dollar is now hostage to our foreign creditors.

- Belying political claims that inflation is under control, the actual consumer price index has shot up 490 percent since 1970.

- While proclaiming that the American consumer has never had it better, many politicians neglect to mention that since 1980, individual tax collections by the government, not including Social Security, have gone up over 350 percent on an annualized basis over the 1970 figure, while the median income has gone up only 240 percent. In other words, taxes have gone up nearly 1.5 times faster than income. This fact helps explain why American installment debt is now over $2 trillion, why it takes two incomes to provide the lifestyle one income provided in the 1960s, the low savings rate, and the stagnant gross national product. If you were to blend Social Security and Medicare payments into that ratio, the gap between income and tax collections would be substantially wider.

Many have concluded that in the face of these seemingly intractable problems, there will be a day of reckoning. The economy has become like the bus in the movie rigged with a bomb. Stop, the terrorist warns, and the bus will be blown to bits. Proceed, and the bus either runs out of gas, in which case it is blown to bits, or ultimately careens out of control with the same result. The massive deficits and national debt continue because, if they suddenly ended, the American economy could not withstand the shock. Yet, if they continue, eventually the American economy ends up either in a deflationary bankruptcy or in an inflationary currency meltdown. As Federal Reserve Chairman Alan Greenspan once stated in congressional testimony, "These trends cannot extend to infinity."

Despite Mr. Greenspan's recurrent warnings, not a single one of these trends shows even a hint of reversing. To the contrary, they seem to be worsening exponentially like a nuclear chain reaction. Rather than acting on these problems, politicians have changed tactics. They now use disinformation, even propaganda, in an attempt to make it appear as if the problems do not exist. Presidential candidate Ross Perot, during the 1992 presidential campaign, colorfully likened the situation to a crazy aunt locked in the attic—the one the neighbors know about, but no one in the family wants to acknowledge.

Let's take the government deficit as an example. From 1999 through 2001, the federal government actually ran a budget surplus for the first time in decades. Receipts topped outlays by roughly $100 and $200 billion annually. That sounded good to most Americans, and the administration of President Bill Clinton greeted the development as a new era in government finance. However, the Clinton administration failed to emphasize that this feat was accomplished not by reduced spending or through better management (although this is what was implied), but by borrowing hundreds of billions from the Social Security fund. By fiscal year end 1997, the accumulated federal debt—what the government actually borrowed to stay in operation—stood at $5.413 trillion. And that bit of juggling of the fiscal books didn't end with the Clinton years.

At the end of fiscal year 2001, with George W. Bush now at the reins of the federal government, the national debt came in at $5.807 trillion. During those three years, the government in reality had added nearly $400 billion to the debt while claiming a surplus of about equal that figure—a miscalculation demonstrating just how far Washington is willing to go to keep the facts from the American people. Neither the Republicans nor the Democrats questioned these figures until the press began to make an issue of it for the 2004 election year—an indication, if not of complicity, then at least of benign neglect. Once again, that crazy aunt in the attic comes to mind. In the pragmatic world of international finance, however, these trends have been enough to cause considerable concern.

The Developing International Currency Crisis

The U.S. dollar is a currency in crisis. Its purchasing power has been eroding in fits and starts since World War II. The 1945 dollar is now worth less than 10 cents. The 1970 dollar is now worth about 21 cents. The 1980 dollar, during a time when Americans were constantly reminded that inflation was "under control," is now worth about 46 cents. Against two of the dollar's most tenacious competitors, the Swiss franc and the Japanese yen, its performance has been dismal.

In 1985, it cost Americans 40 cents to purchase a Swiss franc and 0.4 cents to purchase a Japanese yen. In 2004, it cost 80 cents to buy that same Swiss franc and nearly a full cent to purchase a Japanese yen. In other words, the dollar has lost half its value against two of the world's major currencies over the past twenty years. In short, we are headed the wrong direction on a one-way street. Someday, the oncoming rush could overwhelm us.

Historically, assets denominated in a currency gone bad can be ultimately submerged in a sea of debased paper value, sometimes never to recover—the infamous Nightmare German Inflation of the 1920s being one of the more conspicuous examples. In that notable episode of a currency gone bad, the wholesale inflation index went from one to 726 billion. An individual's life savings could not purchase a loaf of bread or a cup of coffee. People would line up early in the morning to purchase goods they knew would escalate in price by afternoon. Wage earners were paid twice a day and wives would wait at the factory gate for their husbands' paychecks to spend them before prices went up again.

Although the United States has never seen inflation reach that advanced state, the many parallels between 1924 Germany and the present-day United States are cause for concern. Few can look at the constant depreciation of the dollar since the early 1970s and fail to be alarmed that the currency could someday go off the rails. It seems we differ from 1924 Germany only in the duration between cause and effect. Whereas the German experience was compressed over a few short years, ours has been more protracted. This has occurred for two good reasons. First, American central bankers have learned enough from the German experience to delay, extend, and make more tolerable the consequences of excessive money printing. Second, Germany was a small state isolated from the rest of the world, a pariah nation of sorts after the World War I Allied victory. As a result, it had a difficult time finding a market for its government bonds. German deficits had to be financed internally—an impossibility that greatly accelerated the government's printing of fiat currency.

A is for ...

Fiat currency or money is paper money that a government has declared to be legal tender, despite the fact that it has no intrinsic value and is not backed by reserves. Most of the world's paper money is fiat money.

Until recently, the United States enjoyed a strong and unquestioned worldwide demand for its government bonds, so the negative effects of government deficits were subdued. But now, low interest rates and a growing fear among G-7 nations (the United States, Canada, the United Kingdom, Germany, France, Japan, and Italy) that U.S. deficits are out of control has threatened the market for U.S. Treasury securities overseas. Although central banks as a whole have not yet started dumping the dollar, they have slowed their purchases. Should the market outside the United States dry up, the Federal Reserve, like the German central bank in the 1920s, will be forced to monetize an ever-larger portion of the debt to keep the government in operation.

In February 2004, Federal Reserve chairman Alan Greenspan told Congress:

> The imbalance in the federal budgetary situation, unless addressed soon, will pose serious longer-term fiscal difficulties. Our demographics—especially the retirement of the baby-boom generation beginning in just a few years—mean that the ratio of workers to retirees will fall substantially. Without corrective action, this development will put substantial pressure on our ability in coming years to provide even minimal government services while maintaining entitlement benefits at their current level, without debilitating increases in tax rates. The longer we wait before addressing these imbalances, the more wrenching the fiscal adjustment ultimately will be . . .
>
> [G]iven the already-substantial accumulation of dollar-denominated debt, foreign investors, both private and official, may become less willing to ab-

sorb ever-growing claims on U.S. residents. Taking steps to increase our national saving through fiscal action to lower federal budget deficits would help diminish the risks that a further reduction in the rate of purchase of dollar assets by foreign investors could severely crimp the business investment that is crucial for our long-term growth.

Faced with such prospects, the Federal Reserve might exercise the other option, the one Greenspan referred to less than a year earlier in another statement, "It could very well crank up the printing press and flood the economy with money."

The largest deficit during the Richard Nixon years was $23.4 billion; Gerald Ford, $73.7 billion; Ronald Reagan, $221.2 billion; George H.W. Bush, $290 billion; Bill Clinton, $350 billion; George W. Bush, $500 billion (projected). This, to say the least, is a frightening progression. The question arises: How far might our creditors be willing to go in supporting a system of perpetual debt in which the United States is the debtor and they are the creditor holding billions in unbacked paper currency? The future of America, as Mr. Greenspan points out, seems to hang on that question.

In the end, the correlation between deficits and inflation is sacrosanct: deficits lead to inflation, and uncontrolled deficits lead to uncontrolled inflation. Whether or not there will be a Nightmare American Inflation remains to be seen. Let it be said, though, that the trend is not favorable. Those who survived the German debacle did so by purchasing gold and other tangible assets early in the process—one of the more famous proofs of the value of gold as a means to asset preservation.

The Dollar Viewed from Overseas

Meanwhile, the world's financial elite have begun hedging their bets in the event of a full-blown dollar crisis. Some central bankers and finance ministers, for example, talk openly about the evolution of a tricurrency international monetary system, a retreat from the current dollar-based system. The yen would dominate Asian trade, the recently introduced European common currency, the euro, would dominate European trade, and the U.S. dollar would dominate trade in the Western hemisphere. Most Americans are unaware that these sorts of discussions are occurring among moneymen all over the world. Americans are led to believe, instead, that all is well with their currency and their economy.

High-level politicians and academics talk about how the world economy got through the fall of the British pound sterling in the early twentieth century by replacing it with the dollar, and how replacing the dollar could be handled just as judiciously. In other words, a good portion of the world's political and financial elite are politely hinting that the dollar is about to be challenged as the world's sole reserve currency, and following up those words with action. A long list of countries have already begun to replace some of their dollar reserve with euros, a trend likely to gather pace as the problems with the dollar mount.

We have to assume that it is in the best interest of all nations to let the U.S. dollar down gradually, if possible, and indeed the highly publicized national interventions in the currency markets represent attempts to reach that objective. No one—not the politicians, not the central bankers, not the world's financial centers—wants an international monetary crisis. However, this can be entered under the "best laid plans" column. What the world's financial stalwarts want and what the free market provides might be two different things.

Jürg M. Lattman, a Swiss-based investment counselor, sums up concisely the international view of the U.S. dollar:

> The U.S. dollar is still the world's reserve currency, although its dominance has substantially waned since the mid-1970s. The number of countries that peg their currencies to the dollar is down by half to 24. As a reserve currency, the dollar is supposed to be a reliable store of value, yet successive American governments have failed to fulfill

this role. Until the early 1980s, America continued to boast the largest net foreign assets in the world. A decade of massive current account deficits, however, has turned America into the world's largest debtor. As such, the government may be tempted to allow inflation to nibble away at the value of the debt and use *devaluation* to reduce its deficits. Hardly desirable properties for a reserve currency.

Lest you dismiss the importance of such views, keep in mind that Lattman is not alone in this sentiment. This is precisely how many investment professionals and economists viewed the Mexican peso in the months and years prior to its precipitous decline in late December 1994, the Asian currency breakdowns of 1997–1998, and the still unsettled Argentine peso debacle that reached crisis proportions in 2002. Perhaps it would be wise to listen to and acknowledge the steady drumbeat just before an all-out attack begins. Whether we are about to witness the demise of the U.S. dollar is an open question that will be debated heatedly in the weeks and months to come. Suffice it to say, the symptoms and potential are present for a rapid change in the dollar's advantage as a reserve currency. If that occurs, a currency crisis in the United States could develop overnight.

Gold and the 1994 Mexican Peso Debacle: A Lesson in Asset Preservation

An example of how gold protects wealth during a currency crisis can be seen in the December 1994 collapse of the Mexican peso. The now infamous Christmas Surprise began with an announcement that the government had devalued the peso. Investor reaction was immediate. As soon as the devaluation was announced, long lines formed at the banks and sell orders piled up at brokerage firms, as alarmed investors attempted to get their money out of these institutions before they collapsed. A financial panic lurched into motion. Many were frozen out of the equity markets because they had dropped so precipitously. The peso was in a constant state of deterioration.

The inflation rate went to 50 percent immediately and stubbornly stayed at that level. Interest rates soared to 70 percent. Those with credit cards and other interest-sensitive debt teetered on the brink of bankruptcy simply because they couldn't make the interest payments. In the first year following the devaluation, the price of the peso went from 28.5 cents to 14 cents (U.S.). Over the ensuing years the peso continued to deteriorate and now trades in the 10-cent range.

The gold price, on the other hand, went immediately from roughly 1,200 pesos per ounce to 2,500 pesos per ounce—a mirror image of the peso's fall. Over the course of 1995, gold exceeded 3,000 pesos—2.5 times its starting point, living up to its reputation as the ultimate disaster hedge (Figure 2 and 3). Only a proper diversification before the fall effectively insulated some investors from the currency crisis. This, perhaps, is the most important lesson the Mexican example has to offer: A 25 to 30 percent portfolio diversification into gold would have recouped nearly everything that was lost in the peso and equities markets!

Prior to the devaluation announcement, no warning was given the citizenry by the Mexican government or any of the country's major financial institutions. Unfortunately, no financial preparation on the part of the average citizen was possible unless one had the wisdom to diversify into gold, or a currency besides the peso, well before the crisis occurred. I use the word "unfortunately" because, if one lacked the foresight to see in what direction the economy was headed, one was little more than a sitting duck when the devaluation struck. In the same vein, there is little reason to believe that any further strong or rapid deterioration in the U.S. dollar, like the one that began in 2002–2003, will be announced proudly and by way of warning on the evening news. Just as it was in Mexico, the incentive would be to keep any such unraveling, or contingent government plans, under wraps for as long as possible to prevent an all-out currency panic within our borders.

Figure 2. **Dollar/Peso Exchange Rate**

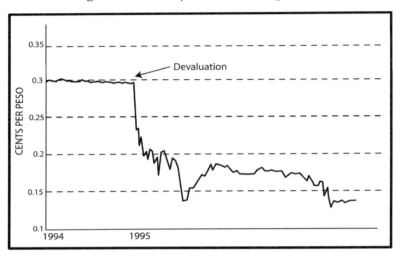

Figure 3. **Gold in Pesos Before
and After Mexican Peso Devaluation**

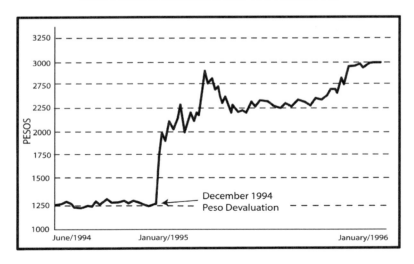

Why Americans Need Gold

If an American currency crisis and economic meltdown were to occur, gold would almost certainly behave much as it did in the Mexican currency crisis. Why? Gold is traditionally viewed by people all over the world as the ultimate money, the historically tested and proven method for protecting wealth in even the most trying circumstances. This will not change. It is a peculiarity of history that we have come to this juncture in the evolution of humanity—particularly in the United States, with all our modern contrivances—and still believe in the transcendence of gold.

Gold has been with us as long as we have sought civilization, freedom, and safety from the financial, political, and social storms that have afflicted civilization since its beginnings. It saved the French during their disastrous currency inflation of the 1790s. And it saved Americans during both the Continental Dollar collapse after the Revolutionary War and the Greenback inflation after the Civil War. The twentieth century has been no exception. Gold was a bulwark during the already mentioned Nightmare German Inflation in the 1920s that paved the way for Adolf Hitler, the many hyper-inflationary blow-offs in South and Central America, the fall of Saigon, and the collapse of the Soviet Union in the early 1990s, as well as the multifaceted Asian Contagion in 1997, and the most recent currency debacle and bank panic in Argentina in 2002. These are only a few of the more memorable occasions when gold played a critical role in asset preservation. Many more instances have ended up on the back burner of history.

Gold today continues to play a critical and central role in the financial planning of the world's central banks and that of countless private investors. The reasons are both simple and practical. Gold affords humanity precisely what it needs from time to time—the protection of wealth against the most threatening circumstances, not the least of which is the destruction of a nation's money by its own government. Perhaps something in our ancestral subconscious places this value on gold. Perhaps it is something in our intellectual grasp of history. Whatever the case, gold has always been in the deepest sense a symbol of wealth, freedom, and endurance. Gold is not at all a primitive and no longer a functional form of wealth, as some of its critics contend, but instead transcendent. If we own it, we not only survive but prevail, to borrow a phrase from William Faulkner. We find comfort in gold. That is why so many of us own it.

In *The New World of Gold*, analyst Timothy Green summed it up this way:

> What John Maynard Keynes called "the barbarous relic" still clings tenaciously to men's hearts. It remains the only universally accepted medium of exchange, the ultimate currency by which one nation, whether capitalist or communist, settles its debts with another . . . The importance governments still attach to gold as an essential bastion of a nation's wealth is more than equaled by ordinary people the world over, who see gold as the sheet anchor against devaluations or the hazards of war . . . Even the U.S. government, despite the many anti-gold pronouncements over recent years, has issued its paratroopers and agents with "escape and evasion" kits in gold. The Atlantic kit includes a gold sovereign, two half sovereigns, a Swiss twenty-franc coin, and three gold rings; the Southeast Asia kit contains a gold chain, a gold pendant, two gold coins, and a gold wristwatch. "The gold is for barter purposes," a Pentagon official explains. Actually, a London bullion dealer put it best: "Gold is bedrock."

Gold: No One's Liability

Gold, it is often said, is the only asset that is not simultaneously someone else's liability. This is a very important concept to grasp. Once you understand it, little else is needed to justify the inclusion of gold in your investment portfolio. When you own a bond, certified deposit, money market, or annuity, you have essentially loaned an individual or an institution your money. To garner a return on that money, you are relying upon someone or something's performance. As compensation for that risk, you are paid interest on your money. Of course, stock values, as we so tellingly have come to realize over the last several years, rely on individual and institutional performance as well. If something goes wrong, the investor is at risk of losing all or part of the investment—as those who held such notable securities as Enron, WorldCom, and Tyco found out when the 1990s stock market bubble succumbed to a meltdown.

Gold, on the other hand, does not pay interest. It does not rely on individual or institutional performance. Therefore, it does not depend on anything other than what it is, itself, for value. If it did, gold owners would be at risk of default.

Those who criticize gold because it fails to offer a return do not really understand gold's position as the fixed North Star of asset value around which all other asset values rotate. Gold is a stand-alone asset. It relies on no individual or institution for value. Gold investors prefer it this way. In the ultimate sense, this is what money is and what money should be. It can always be relied upon when saved or held as a reserve asset in case of an emergency.

Gold will do for Americans, if necessary, what it did for the Vietnamese couple described at the beginning of this chapter, and for the Mexicans, East Asians, and Argentineans who had the wisdom to accumulate it before the various currency disasters swept through those economies. It will do for Americans what it has done for countless others over the centuries. No matter what happens with the dollar, with the overarching debt problem in the United States, with the stock and bond markets, or with the banking system, the owner of gold will find a friend in the yellow metal—something to rely upon when the chips are down. In gold, investors find a vehicle to protect their wealth. Gold is bedrock.

2

B is for…

Bullion Coins: Portable, Liquid, and a Reliable Measure of Value

Do not hold as gold all that shines as gold.
—Alain de Lille

G old for investment purposes is manufactured in two forms: coin or bar. Most of the gold owned by private investors around the world, however, is in the form of coins because of their portability and liquidity, that is, the ease with which they can be converted to cash. A third reason why coins are the preferred vehicle for gold ownership is that the minted coin is a standardized measure of weight and purity upon which current and future owners can rely for value.

One of the first questions most prospective investors ask is, "What should I buy?" The short answer is gold bullion coins like the U.S. Eagle, the Austrian Philharmonic, the South African Krugerrand, and the Canadian Maple Leaf in some combination with pre-1933 small-sized European gold coins and U.S. $20 gold pieces. These items should lay the foundation for any sound money portfolio. Jewelry, artistic objects, or very rare gold collectible coins should not be used for basic asset preservation because their gold value makes up such a small part of their overall value. Gold bullion coins are the safest and best method for protecting wealth and providing insurance against economic calamity. I discuss the reasons for owning the historic gold coins in a later section.

Most Popular Gold Coins

In this chapter, you'll find the most popular gold bullion coins with their weights, purity, and face values (Figure 4). These coins go up and down with the gold price, are dated with their year of manufacture, and trade at a slight premium over the gold value. They can be bought and sold almost anywhere in the world. They are easily recognizable, of standard weight and purity, and can be readily priced based on their gold content. Many first-time investors believe gold is purchased in the form of the bullion bars depicted in the movies, but in the real world most investors buy 1-ounce bullion coins. This is the most popular, most convenient, most liquid, and safest way to own gold. With some exceptions, these coins generally trade among most retail firms at 5 to 8 percent over the gold price. This premium above the gold price consists of wholesale markup, retail markup, and seigniorage. *Seigniorage* is a charge the mint places on the coin to cover manufacturing costs and profits. It usually averages in the 2.5- to 3-percent range. Wholesalers add about 0.5 to 1 percent. Retail brokers and dealers usually add commissions from 1 to 5 percent, depending on the size of your order and other factors.

Along with the standard 1-ounce coins, most of the mints also manufacture gold coins in smaller denominations of ½, ¼, and 1/10 ounce. Because it costs approximately the same amount of money to manufacture any coin no matter the size, the smaller the coin the greater the premium per ounce. You can find current pricing in the financial sections of most local newspapers as well as in the national business and financial newspapers and on Internet sites.

Figure 4. **Commonly Traded Gold Coins**

Austrian Philharmonic

2000 shillings
Gross Weight: 31.103 grams (1 troy ounce)
Fineness: .9999 or 24 karats
Diameter: 37 mm
Fine Gold Content: 31.103 grams (1 troy ounce)
Also Available in ½, ¼, 1/10 ounce

American Eagle

$50
Gross Weight: 33.930 grams (1.0910 troy ounces)
Fineness: .916 or 22 karats
Diameter: 32.7 mm
Fine Gold Content: 31.103 grams (1 troy ounce)
Also Available in ½, ¼, 1/10 ounce

B is for...

Canadian Maple Leaf

$50
Gross Weight: 31.1033 grams
(1 troy ounce)
Fineness: .9999 or 24 karats
Diameter: 30 mm
Fine Gold Content: 31.1033
grams (1 troy ounce)
Also Available in ½, ¼,
1/10 ounce

Australian Kangaroo

$100
Gross Weight: 31.1033 grams
(1 troy ounce)
Fineness: .9999 or 24 karats
Diameter: 32.10 mm
Fine Gold Content: 31.1033
grams (1 troy ounce)
Also Available in ½, ¼,
1/10 ounce

South African Krugerrand

No currency value
Gross Weight: 33.930 grams
(1.0909 troy ounce)
Fineness: .916 or 22 karats
Diameter: 34 mm
Also Available in ½, ¼,
1/10 ounce

The Krugerrand

The first legal tender bullion coin to gain worldwide use in the modern era was the South African Krugerrand, introduced in 1970. To this day, many gold owners equate gold ownership with Krugerrand ownership. The Krugerrand received its first competition from the Canadian Maple Leaf, introduced in 1979. Eventually the Maple Leaf supplanted the Krugerrand as the world's top seller, gaining a significant market share as a 1-ounce pure gold coin.

Most of the competing top gold bullion coins contain one pure ounce of gold, but some are alloyed, which can be confusing for investors. The Krugerrand contains one pure troy ounce, but overall is 0.9167 fine. *Fineness* refers to the pure gold weight per 1,000 parts. A fineness of 0.9167 translates, for example, to 91.67 percent pure gold. Fineness does not refer to the amount of pure gold within the coin, but instead to the overall purity.

Other Gold Coins

In 1986, the U.S. mint introduced the United States Eagle, and the Austrian Philharmonic quickly followed in 1989. The United States Eagle is the most popular bullion with American investors. It is also 0.9167 fine. Like the Krugerrand, the United States Eagle weighs slightly more than one ounce. The Canadian Maple Leaf and Austrian Philharmonic, on the other hand, weigh one ounce and are 0.9999 fine. As mentioned, the key factor is that all four of these coins contain one pure ounce of gold, although they may weigh more than one ounce in total. Therefore, pricing can be readily compared. These four coins dominate the modern bullion coin market.

For the most part, bullion coins present a very stable market for investors. This has been the primary reason for their success. However, an exception occurred in 1984 when the U.S. Congress banned the import of the Krugerrand as part of the economic sanctions imposed on South Africa. The premium dropped to slightly above the gold price and never completely recovered.

The Pricing of Bullion

Gold bullion coins are priced in the United States during the business day using the COMEX in New York as a price basis. COMEX is the leading exchange for gold futures and options in the United States. Prices are set on the floor of the exchange by open outcry. Those prices are then recorded electronically and relayed around the world via the Internet and various quoting services. The price changes constantly during the trading day. After the close, dealers base their pricing on the after-hours ACCESS market price, which also fluctuates continuously. The ACCESS market is an electronic continuation of the COMEX floor trading. Some dealers will allow their better customers to lock in prices over the telephone, but this usually requires that you have an established relationship with the dealer or broker. Some firms will take a credit card number to assure your follow-through on the locked-in price. In lieu of locking in over the telephone, your dealer may require that good funds be on hand—by wire or cashier's check—before your purchase price is set. Upon receiving your funds, dealers will either execute your order at market or contact you before locking in the price, depending upon your wishes. Differences between the amount you send and your actual price are then paid by check before actual delivery.

Bullion coins are available at banks, brokerage firms, gold bullion firms, and coin dealers. Banks have largely withdrawn from this market in the United States, having found it difficult to make the two-way market investors require. A very few of the large Wall Street banks still offer this service. Brokerage firms have never been major players in the gold bullion coin market. In most cases, they have found it difficult to compete price-wise with those who specialize in gold.

Should You Buy Gold Bullion Bars?

Most experts recommend that investors avoid bullion bars. Although the commission and markups are marginally less on bars than on coins, complications come into play when the time comes to sell bullion. Most dealers will want to see the bars before they buy them because of problems with counterfeiting. Some will not buy without an *assay*, a chemical analysis that determines the gold's purity. In most cases, gold firms will not set the resale price until after the bars have been delivered to their location or depository for inspection. This presents difficulties if the client is anxious to capture a price and finds out that it can't be done until after the bars are received by the buyer. Similarly, bullion bars could also present problems for those wishing to trade gold for merchandise in the event of an economic breakdown, because the individual receiving the gold bullion has no way of knowing whether the bars are real or counterfeit.

Because of these trade and exchange difficulties, we counsel our clientele to avoid bullion bars. The marginal added cost on bullion coins is a small price to pay when weighed against the potential disadvantages of owning bars. From the time of Lydia's Croesus, who was the first to mint gold coins (and from whom the legend of the Midas Touch evolved), the coining of gold served to standardize weight and purity and thus to facilitate trade and commerce. Modern gold bullion coins are the descendants of the coins first minted by Croesus.

C is for…
Choosing a Gold Firm

When choosing a gold firm, it is extremely important that you develop a relationship with one that specializes in precious metals and has a history of trading in this market. A strong relationship with a gold firm will facilitate both your buying and selling. It will also play a significant role in how your portfolio is structured.

For the beginning investor, it pays to be cautious in choosing a gold firm because how you start strongly affects how you will finish. Creating a comfort zone in which you can make your gold purchases with a strong degree of confidence and safety should be your primary goal. A logical and commonsense approach would be to interview a few of the major gold firms to find one that is a good fit. The purpose of this chapter is to provide some guidelines to help you achieve that objective.

In addition to allaying concerns about pricing and product selection, a solid, professional gold firm can go a long way in helping the investor shortcut the learning curve and avoid some of the problems and pitfalls encountered along the way.

A Common Investment Mistake

At the outset, the biggest trap investors fall into is buying a gold investment that bears little or no relationship to their objectives. A good example is *safe-haven investors*, a group that makes up about 75 percent of entry-level investors. For the most part, this investor simply hopes to add gold coins to his or her portfolio mix for defensive purposes. Too often, the safe-haven investor ends up instead with a leveraged gold position or a handful of exotic rare coins, often costing five or six figures. High-end U.S. rare coins, futures contracts, leverage schemes, and even gold stock investments, although they serve a purpose, have little to do with safe-haven investing and should be assigned to the risk portion of the overall portfolio. How does this happen? It happens because the investor loses sight of the original objective and allows himself or herself to be drawn into something that has little or nothing to do with why the call was placed in the first place. Don't let that happen to you.

Focus on Your Objective

Gold coins and bullion should primarily be viewed as a portfolio hedge and insurance against a variety of economic and financial uncertainties, an objective that should be secured before moving on to the risk and profit aspect of gold investing. If, at the outset, you find a highly professional gold firm, one that does not have its own agenda, it can help you choose the right gold product mix for your portfolio—one that will serve your interests, not someone else's. By getting with the right gold firm, you are likely to find your gold ownership a very rewarding experience. If you find the wrong one and get into the wrong investment products (as have so many), it could turn your attempt to diversify your portfolio into a disaster. Unbiased, objective advice from one's gold advisor is key to successful participation in the gold market. After that, ongoing market information and education are crucial to your continued success.

Choosing a Gold Firm
Select an Established Firm

Deal only with firms that have been in operation for a number of years. Five years is good; ten years or more is even better. As gold continues its secular bull market, new firms will begin to pop up like the flowers in spring. In fact, this process has already begun with new gold enterprises cropping up on the Internet. Some of them are no more than home-based operations with little or no real experience in the gold market, but their Web sites make them look every bit as appealing as some of the firms that have been around for decades. Some of these online firms will end up being solid, reliable gold sources, but most will fall short. Firms ten years old or more have been around through thick and thin. They are dedicated to the gold market and are usually owned by individuals who are true believers. These are the best firms with which to establish a relationship.

Check Credentials

What are the professional organizations to which the firm belongs? Request written information about the firm. An introductory package goes a long way toward determining what the firm has to offer and whether or not its philosophy is in concert with your own. Do not make your gold purchase until you have exercised due diligence and checked out the firm.

Better Business Bureaus have gone to automated inquiry programs in most areas, which makes it easy to investigate the firm. If the organization is not a member of the Better Business Bureau, this should serve as a warning. If a company has had complaints, it might be worthwhile to check with the Bureau on how those complaints were handled. The existence of a complaint is not proof that you are in contact with a questionable firm. However, if the complaints have not been properly handled, there is cause for concern.

Those who frequent the Internet can check to see if the firm has been approved by the *Better Business Bureau Online Reliability Program*. Strict codes of conduct are associated with the BBB Online Reliability Program. In most cases, the firms that have passed muster display the Better Business Bureau Reliability Program banner on their Web sites. Most of the top gold dealers belong to the *Industry Council for Tangible Assets (ICTA)*. Although ICTA does not rate gold firms or in any way regulate them, it is good for you as a consumer to know how long the firm has been a member. It will confirm their claims of longevity.

Ask about Transaction Details

What does the firm recommend for asset preservation purposes? What does it recommend for speculative profit potential? How should the portfolio be balanced? When is the price set? Is it locked in while your payment is being sent? What premiums are you paying over the gold price? What forms of payment are accepted? How will your gold be shipped? Make sure that your metal is sent either registered and insured by the U.S. Postal Service, or fully insured by private carrier. In both cases, you want to be sure it is being sent "signature required."

Beware of Sales Pitches

If the firm calls you repeatedly, badgers you, or calls with one great deal after another, be careful. There might be something wrong. If they persist in trying to sell you something in which you have no interest or that doesn't fit your needs and goals, this is another red flag. Resist and seek more information and other opinions. Do not make a decision until you have received sufficient information.

Check and Compare Pricing

Cheaper is not always better. In fact, below-market pricing is a bright red flag. If a deal sounds too good to be true, it probably is. When you compare prices, make sure that you are comparing apples to apples. Ask for quotes as a percentage over the gold price. With the pricing moving by the second, price comparisons cannot be done effectively any other way.

Trust Referrals

The best firm to deal with is the one you are referred to by a trusted friend or family member who has experience with that firm. Such experience is invaluable.

Trust Your Instincts

If you go through this process, receive acceptable answers to your questions and you like what you see and hear, go with that firm. If you have the slightest doubt, especially if the firm does not sufficiently meet the criteria above, then go back to square one and start over. Better to be safe than sorry.

Importance of Choosing the Right Firm

First, a firm that has been around for a while can guide you over some of the hurdles. It can also answer your questions quickly and thoroughly. The chances of receiving the correct information are greatly heightened. For most investors, what to buy is the critical question. A good gold broker can put you on the right path after asking just a few questions: Why are you buying gold? What are you thinking about these days to prompt your looking into gold? The broker who doesn't ask such questions is probably inexperienced and is touting what the firm wants him to tout. An interest in you specifically as an investor is an indicator that you might have found a firm worth further investigation.

Second, it is extremely important for most investors to find a firm with which they have a philosophical affinity. A shared viewpoint on economic and political circumstances is a clue that this firm can meet your needs both now and in the future as circumstances change.

Third, a client-oriented company that takes an interest in your gold investment is far preferable to a customer-oriented company. Customer-oriented companies compete primarily on price with little regard to the overall needs of the client. These companies are usually staffed by low-paid employees who essentially serve a clerking function. A question like, "Why are you buying gold?" would never be asked because the objective is to fill the order and move on to the next transaction. You say you want gold coin X. They may sell you gold coin X with little regard to the reasons why you are buying gold or the fact that the coin might not be the best coin for you based on your objectives. Client-based firms are more interested in you as an individual. A good gold broker will ask a few key questions to get a feel for the client. If that occurs, you know you are on the right track.

Last but not least, choosing the right firm is essential to properly managing the long-term nature of your gold holdings. During your time as a gold owner, much is likely to change in the economic and political milieu. You will want to stay informed. The better gold firms usually offer information services like newsletters, and information-based Internet Web sites. In addition, brokers at these firms usually make themselves available for further consultation even after you have made your purchase. Representatives of client-oriented firms usually spend a great deal of time keeping themselves informed.

The gold firm you choose should be an important resource for you as the years go by. You will also want to form a relationship with a firm that will be around for additional purchases and future sales. In short, spend some time choosing a gold firm. Your future as a gold investor depends upon choosing a good one.

4

D is for ...
Diversification: Now More Than Ever

Diversification—distributing one's assets across a spectrum of investment alternatives—is one of the hallmarks of prudent portfolio management. For most, diversification amounts simply to dividing one's available capital among stocks (including mutual funds), bonds, and cash savings. However, if gold is excluded, such a division of assets is superficial at best, because it fails to take into account the corrosive effects of currency depreciation on the overall portfolio.

Chairman of the U.S. Federal Reserve Alan Greenspan has made many favorable comments about gold over the years. Even as chair of the Fed, he has remained one of the most eloquent defenders of gold, a position he has maintained for most of his life. The following comment, given during congressional testimony some years ago, goes to the heart of the issue with respect to gold's overall portfolio role:

> I do think there is a considerable amount of information about the nature of a domestic currency from observing its price in terms of gold. It is a longer-term issue. It is an issue which I think is relevant, and if you don't believe that, you always have to ask the question why it is that central banks hold so much gold which earns no interest and

which costs them money to store. The answer is obvious: they consider it of significant value, and, indeed, they consider it the ultimate means of payment, one that does not require any form of endorsement. There is something out there that is terribly important that the gold price is telling us. I think that disregarding it is to fail to recognize certain crucial aspects of the value of currencies.

Why Buy Gold?

This brief but revealing statement from a man who spends a good part of his day worrying about currency values illustrates the importance of gold in portfolio diversification, for private investors as well as central banks. As a matter of fact, if you were to ask a hundred gold buyers why they own gold, a respectable majority would immediately answer, "For diversification." Most investors equate diversification with peace of mind. Diversification implies preparation for a variety of potential economic events. If the portfolio is properly structured, it matters not if stock markets crash, bonds lose value, or currencies suffer debasement. The hard assets of the portfolio will pick up the slack.

Traditional Swiss money managers, renowned for their ability to handle money and who manage investments for some of the world's wealthiest people, traditionally recommend a diversification into gold of 10 to 20 percent for good reason. Beyond the normal risks of market fluctuations associated with stock and bond investments, there is the additional danger of depreciation in the currency underlying the stock or bond. Denominated in a domestic currency (pesos, yen, euros, and dollars), these investments rely on sound central bank and government currency management policies to maintain their value. It is conceivable that a corporation or municipality, for example, could be perfectly managed, yet its bonds could still erode in value due to politically expedient currency debasement on the part of federal authorities.

D is for ...

Adding Gold to Your Portfolio

Gold diversification makes particularly good sense when stock and bond markets have reached cyclical highs, even if the plateau extends over a period of months or years. In many cases (but not always), gold moves opposite the trend in equities markets. In the late 1990s, when the U.S. stock market was at an all-time high, many investors began to move out of stocks and bonds and into gold with the hope of securing profits garnered in those markets. This strategy paid dividends a few years later when gold shook off its long dormancy and began to rise. Those who failed to diversify saw many of their stocks plummet—some disastrously—although the Dow Jones Industrial Average (DJIA) itself stayed range-bound. In the United States today, gold diversification

Figure 5. **100 Percent Stock Portfolio Versus Initial 70 Percent stocks with 30 Percent Gold Diversification**

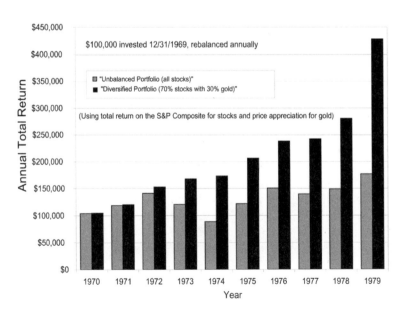

Figure 6. **Inflation-Adjusted Returns 100 Percent Stock Portfolio Versus Initial 70 Percent Stocks with 30 Percent Gold**

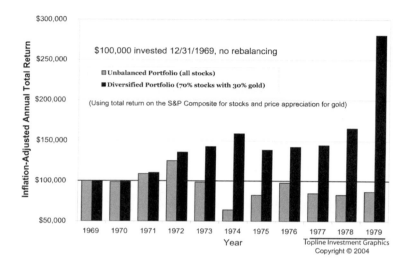

is viewed generally as a commonsense portfolio strategy, and millions include it as part of their investment planning.

For American investors the 1970s, the last long-term bear market in stocks and the dollar, serve as an interesting case study for the power of diversification in the overall investment portfolio. The graph (Figure 5) shows two model portfolios during the 1970s, one invested 100 percent in stocks, and the other invested 70 percent in stocks and 30 percent in gold. Each portfolio started with $100,000. The all-stocks portfolio kept pace with the diversified portfolio until 1972, when both stocks and gold began to react to the dollar devaluation and burgeoning inflation crisis. By 1973, the diversified portfolio (with gold breaking to the upside, pushed by the building inflation rate) was already worth more than the all-stocks portfolio. In the mid-1970s, the 30-percent diversified portfolio nearly doubled in value over the all-stocks portfolio. By 1979, at the peak of the crisis, the gold-diversified portfolio rocketed to nearly $425,000 (more than three times where it started in 1970), while the all-stocks portfolio could manage a value of only $175,000—a meager annualized return on investment over the period studied when you consider that this chart does not take into account the double-digit inflation rate that prevailed over much of the period.

Although the differences between the diversified and nondiversified portfolios were acute even before inflation was taken into account, when the real rate of return is blended into the analysis, the results are even more revealing (Figure 6). Over the course of the 1970s, $100,000 invested in the all-stocks portfolio would have been worth just under $87,000, a real loss of $13,000. The diversified portfolio would have been valued at $280,500 in constant dollars, a real return of $180,000 before taxes.

The accompanying chart amply illustrates the power and value of proper diversification. Gold in the modern era, although it is described, classified, and utilized in many different ways, is still first and foremost portfolio insurance and should be viewed as such. Investors who understand the volatile nature of investment markets under the current fiat money system would be well served to become proactive about gold ownership and not wait for their portfolio advisor to suggest it. Too often that suggestion never comes, and your portfolio ends up looking like the one in our study.

I recommend a gold diversification of 10 to 30 percent of your total assets, not including your residence. The degree of diversification depends completely on your own reading of the economic situation and its potential outcomes. Obviously, the degree to which you diversify is a function of how you gauge prospects for the overall economy. A good starting point is 10 percent of your assets, just in case. From there, your level of commitment should move incrementally higher to match your level of concern, to a maximum of 30 percent. As the charts in this section illustrate, a commitment of 30 percent in the overall portfolio should more than compensate for the negative effects of a bear market in stocks, bonds, and the dollar, and could become a life saver should the worst happen—a major currency crisis and complete financial collapse. Diversify to hedge the financial and economic cycle. Diversify to hedge the ultimate disaster. Diversify with gold.

5

E is for...

Education: The Key to Successful Gold Investing

> *Truth must be ground for every man by*
> *himself out of its husk, with such help as he*
> *can get, indeed, but not without stern labor*
> *of his own.*
> —John Ruskin

During the 1990s, as we all listened to the bubble market psycho-semantics, we lost sight of a very old piece of advice that investment professionals used to offer their clients as a matter of course: Buy the book before you buy the investment. Unfortunately, that loss of focus contributed to millions believing the 1990s mantra that markets and the economy no longer cycled, that we were on a one-way street to perpetual prosperity, and the stock market would never falter again.

Such naiveté cost investors trillions during the subsequent stock market correction. Even a cursory study and understanding of the financial markets and their history might have encouraged a more pragmatic portfolio approach. After all, the history of financial cycles in reality is just as rich in mania, panics, and crashes as it is in bull market triumphs, although only a handful on Wall Street would have subscribed to such anecdotal evidence during the 1990s.

Learn, Then Buy

Remember that old formulation: "The education first, the investment second." In the case of gold, a more proper axiom might be, "Buy the newsletter," or "Surf the World Wide Web" before you buy the investment. Most of the best information on gold—factual, analytical, and opinion—is more readily available through those two sources than at your local bookstore. These venues are also a rich source of "how to" information on gold. This is not to say there are not a few good books and magazine articles available on the subject of gold that you should check out at your local bookstores and libraries. No matter how you obtain your education, it is critical for you to have solid knowledge about gold before making your first purchase.

Sources of Information

Some of the best analytical work today is being done not at the university level, or even in the research departments of the various large Wall Street firms, but instead in two rapidly growing venues for information distribution. First are the independent newsletters; second are investment-oriented Web sites. These include the wire services such as Reuters, Oster Dow Jones and some of the major market news-oriented sites such as Bloomberg and CBS MarketWatch.

In addition, some excellent sites are devoted completely to gold, like USAGOLD.com (the author's Web site), Gold Eagle.com, and Kitco.com. The widespread availability of information and research data through computerization has created a whole new intellectual community no longer tied to university libraries or corporate databases.

Also, the modern analyst equipped with a personal computer and rapid access to vast information resources is not restrained institutionally. These sources quite often produce not only interesting material, but also enormously useful work for "seekers of truth." When you bring the World Wide Web into the mix, that information is made available to the public in rapid fashion—an enormous advantage that at one time was only available within large financial and educational organizations. Keep in mind that both the best gold Web sites and the top newsletter writers are offering their opinion. Sometimes they are right; sometimes they are wrong. Their views are quite often controversial and at times off the beaten path. You are the final arbiter and decision maker. Read carefully, analyze, and form you own opinion.

You can get good, although sanitized, day-to-day information through your local newspaper, financial publications, and TV news—particularly the business television channels where information on gold appears regularly. Many think it is fair to say that the traditional press, with a few exceptions, has a strong antigold bias. This must be taken into account. Another good source of general information and opinion is talk radio. Talk radio may be one of the last bastions of free thought in America. No matter what your political persuasion, these shows can be a good source of information, much of which you are unlikely to find in the traditional media.

The challenge of the twenty-first century and the next phase of the Information Age will be to find, segregate, absorb, and utilize large amounts of information. With respect to investments, the quality of the information you get and your own analytical abilities in processing it will be the difference between success and failure. This holds true not only for your rationale with respect to gold, but also for which investments you choose and the timing required on each. Strategy and overall portfolio design will weigh more heavily in your success than the latest hot tip or follow-the-crowd psychology driven by the mainstream press. Newsletters and the burgeoning Internet with its multiplicity of sources will become an even more vital resource in the years to come. These are sources you will not want to be without.

6

F is for…

Fundamentals: Supply and Demand

Supply and demand tables are the types of dry economic statistics that people usually try to avoid like the latest flu virus. But before you fast-forward through this section, keep in mind that most experts believe the current unusually strong supply-demand fundamentals will be the engine that drives the secular bull market in gold for many years into the future. If asset preservation or wealth protection provides the basic motivation for gold ownership, then profit potential could be an extremely attractive sidebar to gold's story as we progress through the first decade of the twenty-first century.

To be sure, understanding the fundamental relationship between how much gold is being produced (the international supply) and how much is being consumed (the international demand) will be the key to making you an informed and confident gold investor in the future. Many gold analysts now believe gold will exceed its previous high of $875 per ounce sometime in the first decade of the twenty-first century. Such optimism is based not only on the burgeoning economic and dollar crisis (which is formidable in its own right), but also on a convergence of supply and demand factors as outlined below.

Figure 7. World Gold Supply and Demand (in tonnes)

	1993	1994	1995	1996	1997	1998	1999	2000	2001	2002	2003
Supply											
Mine production	2,291	2,285	2,291	2,375	2,493	2,542	2,574	2,591	2,623	2,587	2,601
Official sector sales	468	130	167	279	326	363	477	479	529	556	591
Old gold scrap	577	621	631	644	626	1,099	608	609	708	835	940
Net producer hedging	142	105	475	142	504	97	506	-	-	-	-
Implied net disinvestment	-	203	92	102	275	-	-	357	61	-	-
Total Supply	**3,478**	**3,344**	**3,657**	**3,541**	**4,223**	**4,102**	**4,165**	**4,036**	**3,920**	**3,978**	**4,133**
Demand											
Fabrication											
Jewelry	2,559	2,640	2,812	2,856	3,311	3,182	3,154	3,232	3,038	2,689	2,547
Other	491	455	502	485	562	566	591	560	483	486	507
Total Fabrication	3,050	3,095	3,314	3,341	3,873	3,749	3,745	3,792	3,522	3,175	3,054
Bar hoarding	182	249	343	200	350	163	266	230	248	252	178
Net producer hedging	-	-	-	-	-	-	-	15	151	423	310
Implied net investment	246	-	-	-	-	191	154	-	-	128	591
Total Demand	**3,478**	**3,344**	**3,657**	**3,541**	**4,223**	**4,102**	**4,165**	**4,036**	**3,920**	**3,978**	**4,133**
Gold Price (London PM, US$/oz)	359.82	384.15	384.05	387.87	331.29	294.09	278.57	279.11	271.04	309.68	363.32

Source: Gold Fields Mineral Services, London, United Kingdom: www.gfms.co.uk

Totals may not add up due to independent rounding. Net producer hedging is the change in the physical market impact of mining companies gold loans, forwards and options positions. Implied net investment is the residual from combining all other GFMS data on gold supply/demand as shown in the Summary Table. As such, it captures the net physical impact of all transactions not covered by the other supply/demand variables.

Gold Supply

The total supply of gold for 2003, as shown in the accompanying table (Figure 7), supplied and republished with the permission of Gold Fields Mineral Services (GFMS), was 4,133 tonnes. Of that, 2,601 tonnes came from the world's gold mines, 591 tonnes from the official sector (i.e., the central banks), and 940 tonnes from processing old scrap. The mines then are the primary source, supplying over 60 percent of the gold used annually, with scrap production and the official sector playing secondary roles. The mines supply gold in two ways—first, from ordinary production, and second, from forward selling.

Gold Mine Production around the World

Most of the action in mining exploration these days is occurring in Central and South America, Russia, and western Africa. China, now the fourth largest gold producer, is increasing production, presenting some interesting possibilities for the future.

South Africa, according to GFMS figures, reigns as the world's leading producer of gold (roughly 15 percent of the 2,601 tonnes total), and has enjoyed that distinction longer than most people can remember. The United States (11.5 percent) is second. Australia (10 percent) ranks third, while China (7.8 percent) recently displaced Russia (7.0 percent) in 2002 for fourth. Although South Africa has been the dominant gold producer for decades, its production has been in continuous decline due to a combination of labor problems and aging mines.

Mining in South Africa

In the 1970s, South Africa averaged 1,000 tonnes production per year. By 1985, production had fallen to under 700 tonnes, and by the early twenty-first century, to under 400 tonnes per year. Other producing nations, most notably the United States, Australia, and China, have stepped in to pick up the slack. Some experts project the United States will overtake South Africa in gold production before the decade is out.

Others disagree, citing stiff environmental laws in the United States.

Mining in the United States

The United States holds its lofty position in the mine production rankings due principally to the default of the old Soviet Union and the discovery and development of massive gold reserves in Nevada. The strong increase in production since the 1980s is of more than passing historic interest to gold investors, if for no other reason than to try to assess whether this growth has peaked. In the mid-1990s, U.S. gold production began to decline, and leveled as the decade progressed to the 300- to 350- tonne range. In 2002, production dipped below the 300-tonne level for the first time since the Nevada discoveries. Overall, mining in the United States is problematic. Pressure from environmental and agricultural groups, along with local and state governments, continues to act as a brake on the expansion of the industry.

Over the past three years, for example, four counties in Colorado known for their gold production in times past (Summit, Gilpin, Gunnison and Costilla) have banned the use of cyanide heap leaching, a move being heavily challenged in the courts by the mining industry. If such a ban were passed in Nevada, where already environmental groups are agitating for larger trust fund contributions to safeguard the environment, a significant portion of the U.S. gold production would be removed from the supply-demand tables. As a result, many mining companies are concentrating their exploration capital in more hospitable environs outside the United States.

Mining in Russia

Russia, once the second-largest gold producer in the world, has suffered labor and production problems of its own and has slipped to number five. Since the collapse of the Soviet Union, fundamentals tables list the former republics separately. Consider Uzbekistan and Russia, which together accounted for over 90 percent of the former Soviet Union's production. Comparison shows that supply from the republics of the former Soviet Union has dropped considerably.

Where is Mining Headed?

Above and beyond the various political and environmental problems besieging the gold mining industry internationally, some experts worry that mine production is likely to decline overall due to a decade of exploration budgets having been trimmed to the bone. A lead time of up to ten years is needed between the time that an ore body is located, mapped, and permitted, and actual production. During the 1990s, the low gold price forced mining companies to cut back on exploration in an attempt to balance falling revenues. The gold market is now paying the price for those cutbacks as we head into the second half the decade in the form of static to falling production. High-grade pockets in many cases were mined in the 1990s, and now the mining companies are forced to pull lower grade ore.

In mid-2003, Mineweb.com, a Web site devoted to gold mining, quoted South African mine company CEO Bernard Swaepoel as saying that for a "cocktail of reasons . . . we [the industry] won't be able to mine enough gold to supply the market going forward." Indeed, when one compares production to fabrication needs over the past decade, one can discern an interesting trend—the gap is widening quickly, and although fabrication needs are likely to continue growing over the next several years, mine production is likely to remain static at best, or in the worst case go into severe decline (see Figure 8).

Mine Company Forward Selling

The second way mine companies contribute to the supply is through *forward sales* or *hedging*. Although somewhat complicated, the nuances of forward selling are very important for investors to understand. The two principal players in forward selling are the mines and the central banks. For the mines, forward selling is a convenient and inexpensive form of mine financing. For the central banks, it is a way to make interest on an otherwise dormant balance sheet item. Through a bullion bank intermediary, the mines borrow gold from a central bank and promise to repay the loan from production at a future date.

Some mine company forward sales contracts stretch out over years, sometimes up to a decade. The mining company sells the loaned gold on the open market and uses the proceeds either to finance mining operations or to purchase higher-yielding instruments in a financial operation called a *carry-trade*. The bottom line for the gold market is that, in either instance, forward selling gets gold to the market that would not have been available otherwise, thus creating extraordinary downward pressure on the price.

Once the production is sold forward, it cannot be sold again. If the gold price were to begin rising, as it did in 2002 and 2003, the company not only loses money on its hedge book, the value of its stock is hurt as well.

Figure 8. **Gold Fabrication and Gold Mine Production (Worldwide 1993 to 2003)**

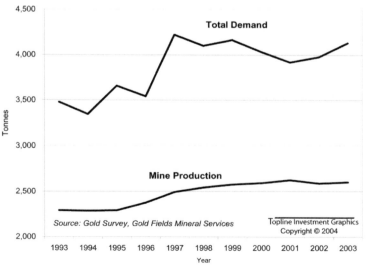

Source: Gold Survey, Gold Fields Mineral Services

Topline Investment Graphics
Copyright © 2004

During the most recent bull market in gold stocks, non-hedged, or marginally hedged miners outperformed the strongly hedged companies by an embarrassingly wide margin. In 2004 with gold trading in the $400 range, one major gold mining company announced that it had suffered a nearly $1.75 billion loss due to its massive hedge book. It subsequently vowed to reduce the firm's exposure to gold's upside through a process known as dehedging. *Dehedging*—buying gold on the open market and using it to repay gold loans early—is the opposite of hedging.

Forward selling in recent years has come under severe attack from sophisticated gold stock investors, who see it as contrary to the purpose of a mining company. "Why," ask these shareholders, "are we involved in financing operations that essentially act to hold down the price of the very commodity we are in the business of producing?" This common-sense complaint has had an impact on management in key gold mining companies and their response has been to begin reversing their hedge books. The very same gold mining companies that added an average of 200 tonnes per year to supply over the past decade instead have added 500 tonnes to demand over the past two years.

Remove that supply from the tables and you have a runaway gold price. Indeed, most gold market experts credit the reversal in mine company hedging practices as key to gold's increase from $250 to $430 since late 1999. Because of the hefty hedge books accrued by mining companies during the 1990s the probability of even more dehedging in the future remains strong. The tonnage to come from this new demand category could well take the market by surprise and contribute to the bullish argument for gold for several years to come.

Official Sector Lending

Central banks contribute to the supply side of the fundamentals in two important ways: Outright sales, and the little-understood process of gold leasing, or lending. When a central bank lends a mining company or financial institution gold, that metal is sold in the market, thus having the same effect as an official sector sale. According to the *Gold Avenue Encyclopedia (GAE)*, some 80 central banks have provided 4,650 tonnes to the lending market over the years. In 1993, that figure stood at roughly 2,000 tonnes.

The current leasing pool encompasses the equivalent of nearly two years' output from the world's gold mines. According to the GAE, "Initially, leasing often came from central banks in developing countries, eager for some return on gold but, increasingly, major European central banks, including the Austrian, Belgian, Netherlands, German and UK central banks, came to participate. Even the Swiss National Bank joined in. GFMS estimates that between 1995 and 1999 over 60 percent of new leasing came from European central banks." As noted earlier, this lending fueled the mine company forward selling boom of the 1990s, with a smaller portion going to various hedge funds and other financial institutions engaged in various carry-trade operations.

It was predictable that at some point the central banks involved in gold lending might reach their limits with respect to the prudent management of gold reserves. Leased gold would then disappear from the supply-demand tables, or at least be severely reduced. That is precisely what happened in 1999, when Europe's top central banks put a crimp in the freewheeling atmosphere in the lending market by signing the Central Bank Gold Agreement, which regulated the amount of gold central banks could lend and/or sell. The rapid growth in the lease pool between 1989 and 1999, and the threat its repayment eventually might have posed for the bullion bank underwriters, could well have been one of the hidden reasons for that landmark gold agreement.

Official Sector Sales

Central bank selling has been a constant on the supply side for decades and will likely continue to be for the foreseeable future (see Figure 9). Most gold market analysts and traders, in fact, see sales as a necessary component of the supply side of the gold fundamentals table. However, a close examination of the chart reveals that central bank gold sales were never the threat to actual tonnage sold that the financial press made them out to be.

For the most part, it wasn't so much the sales themselves (most conducted quietly out of the limelight, the highly publicized Bank of England auctions excepted) that damaged gold sentiment in the late 1990s and early 2000s, but the nearly continuous threat of sales, and the subsequent trumpeting of

Figure 9.
**Net Official Sector Sales
1992 to present
(in tonnes)**

1992	662
1993	468
1994	130
1995	167
1996	279
1997	326
1998	363
1999	477
2000	479
2001	529
2002	556
2003	591

Source: Gold Fields Mineral Services, Ltd.
London, United Kingdom

that threat on the financial pages of the world's newspapers that acted as a deterrent to a rising gold price. If fact, the market absorbed whatever gold was sold with little difficulty, and although the sales usually exerted some passing, short-term pressure on the price, the long-term effects of central bank sales were negligible.

By way of historic perspective, from 1965 to 1975, the Anglo-American countries (the United States, the United Kingdom, Canada, and Australia) were the primary sellers of gold, with the United States and the United Kingdom at the international forefront and Europe for the most part, remaining on the sidelines. In 1965, the Anglo-American countries held nearly 16,000 tonnes of gold in reserve. By 1975, those holdings had been pared to 10,000 tonnes, with the United States suffering the greatest drain. Most of that gold was expended in defense of the dollar and the $35-per-ounce post–World War II benchmark. Europe, on the other hand, held 18,000 tonnes on reserve in 1965 and 17,000 tonnes in

1975. So Europe participated little, if at all, in the pre-1975 dis-gorging of gold from official reserves.

From 1975 through the mid-1990s, the European and Anglo-American countries lost about 1,000 tonnes each from their reserves. Much of that went to Asian countries, which accumulated 1,500 tonnes. Even so, the 500 tonnes that trick-led into the private sector over this 20-year period were far from the avalanche intimated by the financial press. In 1992, net official sales of gold peaked at 622 tons, then quickly fell to a low of 130 tonnes in 1994. From there, official sector sales trended upward until 2003, and thereafter remained between 450 and 590 tonnes. Much of the official sector selling in the early and mid-1990s occurred to meet the requirements of the new European Monetary Union (EMU) as mandated by the Maastricht Treaty. Most of that official sector selling came from Belgium and the Netherlands, two countries with heavy debt loads needing to be reduced before EMU entry. Canada, Australia, and a handful of smaller central banks sold gold in amounts that had little, if any, effect on the market price.

In 1999, when the Bank of England announced that it would auction off a significant portion of its gold reserve, os-tensibly to reinvest the proceeds in interest-bearing dollar- and euro-based securities, gold dropped precipitously from the $330 to the $250 range. However, even though the sales were heavily publicized, the downside was short-lived and the Bank of England thereafter suffered the embarrassment of selling nearly 60 percent of its remaining 715-tonne gold re-serve at less than $300 per ounce. At the time of the sale, Par-liamentarian Sir Henry Tapsell echoed the sentiments of many within the United Kingdom:

> The whole point about gold, and the quality that makes it so special and almost mystical in its appeal, is that it is universal, eternal and almost in-destructible. The Minister will agree that it is also beautiful. The most enduring brand slogan of all time is, "As good as gold." The scientists can clone sheep, and may soon be able to clone humans, but

they are still a long way from being able to clone gold, although they have been trying to do so for 10,000 years. The Chancellor [of the Exchequer, Gordon Brown] may think that he has discovered a new Labour version of the alchemist's stone, but his dollars, yen and euros will not always glitter in a storm and they will never be mistaken for gold.

As mentioned earlier, such sales were abruptly capped by the signing of the Central Bank Gold Agreement. Although we still do not know the full political and economic motivations behind the sales (few believed that the Bank of England was selling gold to buy currencies that were paying historically low interest rates), nation-states rarely sell gold because they want to. They almost always sell gold because economic and/or financial conditions necessitate it.

The Central Bank Gold Agreement: A Watershed Event for the Gold Market

When central bankers representing the nations of Europe signed the Central Bank Gold Agreement in September 1999, George Milling-Stanley of the World Gold Council spoke for many in the gold industry:

> It is important to recognize that the agreement represents something of infinitely greater significance than a mere repetition of statements central bankers had already made, or a clarification of positions they already held. This is a binding agreement, signed by central bank governors on behalf of their respective institutions and/or governments . . . This should finally put to rest the fear that has kept the gold market in its paralyzing grip for years, the fear that central banks have abandoned gold as a reserve asset, and are planning to sell all that they have... That fear flew in the face of all the observable evidence. It is a matter of fact that only five governments have sold a significant quantity of

gold in the past 10 years, if we define a significant quantity as 100 tonnes or more.

The agreement went much deeper than simply control-ling central bank gold sales; it also curtailed the leasing of gold and central bank involvement in the futures and options markets. The announcement sent the price surging from $250 per ounce to well over $300 in a matter of days. Although gold settled down shortly thereafter, many gold analysts point to the signing of the Central Bank Gold Agreement and its strict controls on the supply of gold coming out of the central banks as the watershed event that inaugurated the new, secular bull market in gold.

Haruko Fukuda, at the time Chief Executive Officer for the World Gold Council, spoke eloquently on the subject at the Denver Gold Group conference that year:

> On Sunday 26th September—just three weeks ago—a new era dawned for gold. For the first time in almost exactly 28 years, since convertibility of gold into U.S. dollars for official holders was sus-pended on 15th August 1971, the governments with the largest gold holdings made a positive joint statement on gold. Those three decades have been a period in which gold was persistently sidelined by the official sector attempting to demagnetize gold. In recent years the market has been plagued by persistent rumors of ever increasing official sec-tor sales and each and every announcement of sale by central banks has acted as a trigger for a new downturn in the price of gold. Yet the amount of gold held in reserve by the official sector has barely declined during that period—a decline of a mere 6 percent in three decades.
>
> The Central Bank Gold Agreement was sim-ple, but direct:
>
> 1. Gold will remain an important element of global monetary reserves.

2. The above institutions will not enter the market
    as sellers, with the exception of already decided
    sales.
3. The gold sales already decided will be achieved
    through a concerted program of sales over the
    next five years. Annual sales will not exceed
    approximately 400 tonnes and total sales over this
    period will not exceed 2,000 tonnes.
4. The signatories to this agreement have agreed not
    to expand their gold leasings and their use of
    gold futures and options over this period.
5. This agreement will be reviewed after five years.

Signatories to the agreement were: The European Central Bank, Austria, Belgium, Finland, France, Germany, Ireland, Italy, Luxembourg, the Netherlands, Portugal, Spain, Sweden, Switzerland, and the United Kingdom. Japan, although not a signatory, publicly endorsed the agreement the following day. The United States, also not a signatory, also endorsed the agreement. (Neither the United States nor the International Monetary Fund (IMF) lend gold.)

In March 2004, the signatories renewed the agreement for an additional five years with one changed provision: They increased the amount of gold to be sold over the five-year period from 2,000 to 2,500 tonnes, a relatively benign change. The new agreement was generally greeted in the gold market as a positive development, with some commentators wondering whether the central banks would be able to muster enough gold to meet the 2,500-tonne objective. The most important aspect of the agreement, the fact that sales and leasing activity are, in fact, capped and of known quantity, remains in place.

The Combined Effects of Official Sector Sales and Leasing on the Gold Price

Since the early 1960s, central banks have attempted, with varying levels of success, to impose their will on the gold market. In most instances, that imposition was directed toward keeping the price in check either by selling the metal outright, as was the case in the 1960s and 1970s, or through a combination of sales and leases, as began in the late 1980s. As such, this demonstrates the quantifiably inverse relationship between official sector sales and leases and the gold price. When the intervention (for lack of a better word) is in progress, the price is restrained. When the intervention is abandoned, the price begins rising more quickly than it would under normal circumstances because of built-up price pressure.

This explains the spikes that characterize and dominate the gold charts. Had the official sector not been a seller/lender, price increases would have been gradual and less dramatic, the product of the normal interrelationship between buyers and sellers in a free market. Quite possibly, the run-ups that did occur, particularly the two spikes in the 1970s, would have been more subdued and stretched over a longer period of time.

In the 1960s through the London Gold Pool (with the United States as primary contributor), and again in the mid-1970s through the International Monetary Fund (IMF) and U.S. Treasury sales, the United States made massive interventions in the gold market to keep the price from reflecting dollar weakness. The London Gold Pool was formed in 1961, first to address an attack on the dollar that took the gold price to $40. In 1962, the Pool was again called to respond to the massive demand for gold associated with the Cuban Missile Crisis. By the late 1960s, with the U.S.-government-mandated price still at $35 per ounce, the London Gold Pool was abolished, but not until thousands of tonnes of gold left central bank coffers for the private sector. U.S. gold reserves were reduced from 20,000 tonnes in the 1950s to 9,000 tonnes by 1970.

Shortly thereafter, in 1971, the United States was forced to suspend convertibility and devalue the dollar. Floating exchange rates were introduced. Gold immediately began to rise, hitting $200 in 1974—a nearly sixfold increase over the $35 benchmark, and the first of the spikes mentioned at the top of this section. Again in the mid 1970s, the United States, this time with the help of the IMF, entered the gold market as sellers with over 500 tonnes expended from the U.S. Treasury and nearly 800 tonnes from IMF coffers in the form of direct sales, and an equal amount as returned quotas to various members. Gold was driven back to the $100 level. That plan ran its course by 1978, and once the intervention was lifted, gold resumed its uptrend, culminating in the record $875 price by 1980. Understandably, the better portion of gold returned to IMF members became a part of national reserves and didn't again see the light of day until the late 1980s and the advent of aggressive gold leasing programs and controlled sales.

In those early instances of intervention in the gold market, the primary interest of interventionists was to hold down gold so that U.S. policies with respect to the dollar would not become suspect. Dollar inflation was bubbling just beneath the surface. Monetary and government officials acted to keep the price of gold down so that the dollar would not come under further attack. Once the intervention was abandoned, gold found its natural price level. These stratagems conducted by the central banks, usually with the Bank of England and the Federal Reserve Bank of New York in the lead, never kept gold from eventually achieving its desired level vis-à-vis the dollar. They were simply delaying actions just prior to a full retreat. Essentially, the war was lost before it was even fought.

In the 1990s, the central banks, knowingly or not, were engaged in another protracted battle in the war against gold, only this time through leasing as well as selling programs. Over the past decade, the central banks put nearly 7,000 tonnes of gold on the market. According to GFMS statistics this involved roughly 4,650 tonnes in the form of sales and 2,300 in the form of leases. Through the 1990s, the net effect has been to keep the price of gold under $400 per ounce and for part of the decade under $300 per ounce. With the advent of the Central Bank Gold Agreement in 1999, this most recent intervention has been contravened and regulated.

Gold, in 1999, immediately reacted to the agreement by spiking higher. Prior to the agreement, gold was trading at $260; after September 1999, it broke through $300 and topped out at $339. After a consolidation period and a return to the $260 level, gold began a steady climb that stalled at the $400 level, where it trades as this is written. With the supply of gold throttled, whether or not another spike will develop in the first decade of the twenty-first century depends on developments on the other side of the fundamentals' ledger: gold demand.

Demand for Gold

According to GFMS listings (Figure 7), the demand side of the fundamentals table encompasses three large groupings: jewelry and other fabrication at 3,054 tonnes, or 74 percent of the total; investment at a surprising 769 tonnes (591 tonnes in implied net investment and 178 tonnes in bullion bar purchases), or 14 percent of the total; and producer dehedging at 310 tonnes, about 7.5 percent of the total. A large portion of the jewelry fabrication is considered a safe-haven investment in East and South Asia, so it is difficult to separate jewelry as a monetary asset from that which is used for adornment. In general, worldwide demand has increased by roughly 20 percent over the past decade. There is little on the horizon to prevent this growth trend from extending into the twenty-first century. In fact, these trends could accelerate markedly if accompanied by continued currency problems, particularly with the dollar, investment demand growth, and continued producer dehedging.

Fabrication of Gold

Fabrication demand has remained relatively level over the past decade, in the range of 2,500 to 3,000 tonnes. However, jewelry off-take continues to underpin the demand side of the gold market, rising whenever the dollar price falls and declining whenever it rises. As such, it has become something of a constant, a backdrop against which the rest of the demand side of the equation operates. This picture of relative stability could be radically altered over the coming years as Mainland China moves to liberalize its gold market. The rest of East Asia and the Pacific Rim could also enjoy a revival in fabrication demand as these economies recover from the Asian Contagion of the late 1990s.

Central Bank Gold Purchases

In late 2003, reports of elements within the Chinese financial bureaucracy pushing for a government-sanctioned gold acquisition program began to surface. Thus far, nothing concrete has been announced, but gold market sources in Asia believe that China could enter the market as an official buyer at any time, using the huge reserve disparity between its dollar and gold reserve allocations as a justification. In early 2004, the Japanese Minister of Finance, Sadakazu Tanigaki, stunned financial markets by saying, "it would be wise if Japan brought its gold holdings towards the levels more consistent with those of the other industrialized nations. (For example, Japan holds about 2 percent of its reserves in gold, and Europe holds over 40 percent in gold.) That statement, along with similar statements from Chinese monetary authorities in recent months, amounts to a warning shot across the bow for gold market participants—official sector purchases of gold from the two Asian economic giants are a distinct possibility in the years to come.

Investment Demand

Investment demand is considered by many analysts to be the major X-factor in the fundamentals tables. Since many international investors see gold and the dollar as primary competitors, gold demand tends to rise as the dollar weakens. These trends tend to play out over periods of years, not months, with the ten-year bull market of the 1970s remaining the most telling example of that synergy. During strong dollar years, gold net disinvestment dominated the charts. In 2002 and 2003, with the dollar selling off in international markets, the table has swung in gold's favor, with 137 tonnes net gain in 2002 and a remarkable 591 tonnes net gain for investment demand in 2003. Internationally, private investors, investment funds, and high-net-worth investors who have already purchased gold stand at the vanguard of a trend that could last for some time, given the dollar fundamentals discussed previously. Should the dollar outlook continue to cloud the viability of investment markets across the spectrum and around the world, we could see the influx of private investors from Europe, the United States, and Japan multiply geometrically. This would put heavy pressure on available coin and bullion supplies. In 2002 and 2003, the strong investment market for gold more than made up for the static demand in jewelry fabrication.

Tocqueville Funds' erudite John Hathaway tells in this short analysis why strong and rising gold investment demand could very well be with us for some time to come:

> There are two reasons to invest in gold. First, there is the simple and obvious prospect that it may rise in price and thereby create positive returns for those of us who hold it or gold mining shares. The second reason is not quite so obvious, but it is more powerful. It is the fact that gold's behavior is uncorrelated to other financial assets including bonds, stocks and currencies. When expected returns on financial assets are low, money flows in the direction of gold. It is also true that gold, being uncorrelated as opposed to inversely correlated, can rise while financial asset prices are also rising. It is these characteristics that qualify gold as a form of financial insurance... Gold at $400 is one of the few remaining bargains in a financial world that is a minefield of risk. Investors owe thanks to the central banks. Their repeated sales of the metal have kept a lid on the price. Without such sales, the price would already be several hundred dollars higher. Those with vast pools of wealth to protect, including institutional and private investors, can only hope that these outdated bureaucracies, managed

by financially ignorant civil servants, continue their divestment process to facilitate acquisition of meaningful gold positions at attractive prices . . . The bull market in gold is well underway. While it will suffer periodic setbacks, it will not reach its completion until world governments restore integrity to financial instruments beginning with paper money. There is little to suggest that such a moment is within view.

Conclusion

Now you have a basic understanding of what makes the gold market tick. This brief outline of a very complex subject is in no way meant to be a comprehensive analysis of the supply and demand fundamentals of gold. Whole volumes have been devoted to this analysis. My purpose has been to provide a basic introduction to the interplay of these statistics, mostly provided by Gold Fields Mineral Services, with my own interpretations and conclusions.

To sum up the fundamental picture for gold: accelerating demand and decelerating mine production combined with curtailed central bank involvement on the supply side presents an opportunity unlike anything that has occurred in the gold market since the United States abandoned its interventionist gold policies in the 1970s. As a gold investor, whenever you begin to doubt the long-term viability of gold, return to the fundamentals for a refresher course. It is here that you will find the basic reasons why gold is becoming a standard not only in private investment holdings, but in the world's public treasuries as well.

7

G is for…

Government Debt: Is the United States Going the Way of Mexico and Argentina?

*A democracy cannot exist as a permanent form
of government. It can only exist until the voters discover that
they can vote themselves money from the public treasury.
From that moment on the majority always votes for the
candidates promising the most money from the public
treasury, with the result that a democracy always collapses
over loose fiscal policy followed by a dictatorship. The
average age of the world's great civilizations has been two
hundred years. These nations have progressed through the
following sequence: from bondage to spiritual faith,
from spiritual faith to great courage, from courage to liberty,
from liberty to abundance, from abundance to selfishness,
from selfishness to complacency, from complacency
to apathy, from apathy to dependency, from dependency
back to bondage.*

—Alexander Tyler

The Scottish historian Tyler was talking about ancient Athens when he penned the famous quote above in his *Fall of a Republic*, but he could have been talking about the United States in the late twentieth and early twenty-first cen-

Figure 10. **Gross U.S. Federal Government Debt**

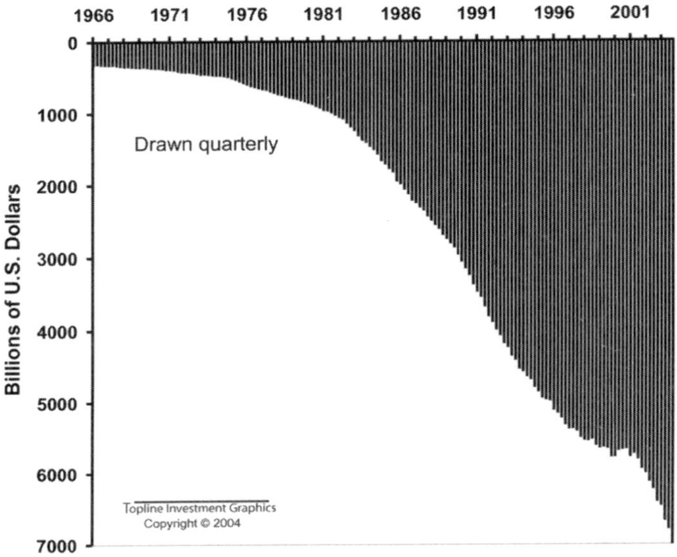

turies. For those with an understanding of the current economic situation in the United States, Tyler's progression carries an unsettling ring of familiarity. The national debt—now over $7 trillion and growing exponentially—lies at the heart of what ails this country, and that debt most certainly originates with the electorate and special interests voting themselves largest from the public treasury (see Figure 10). Your understanding of this problem and what you can do to protect yourself against the seemingly inevitable historic processes it threatens to ignite will be critical to your financial well-being in the years to come.

U.S. Debt

The 1994 Mexican devaluation, as pointed out in Chapter 1, illustrates what could be expected if the debt problem were to get out of control in the United States. The United States is following along the same profligate path of Mexico and Argentina—budget deficits, unconscionable growth in overall public and consumer debt, abnormal increases in foreign-held debt, currency inflation, and so forth. These economic ills characterize the U.S. economy today just as they did the Mexican and Argentinian economies before their respective devaluations and collapses.

As mentioned briefly in an earlier chapter, what has saved this country from a similar fate has been the dollar's unique position as the world's reserve currency. Because other countries are willing to hold the dollar in their treasuries as a reserve item, the United States has thus far escaped full market retribution. Take away the reserve currency advantage and the United States could very well tumble into the same financial abyss that wreaked havoc in Argentina and Mexico.

Dr. H. J. Witteveen, former director of the International Monetary Fund, explained the dollar reserve phenomenon this way:

> This system [the dollar standard] can be criticized, because foreign exchange reserves are created as a consequence of balance of payment deficits of the United States without any relationship to world reserve needs. Implicit in this is an unfair advantage to the reserve country, the United States, because it can finance its deficits by paying in its own currency. This makes it too easy to run deficits, and it creates an inflationary element in the monetary system, compared to the classical gold standard . . . By paying in its own currency, the United States could continue to finance enormous deficits without being forced to introduce adequate deficit reducing measures.

This apparent uneasiness on the part of the international dollar holders raises some serious questions, most importantly, "What might happen to the typical American investment portfolio, should the dollar's reserve status diminish radically?"

Figure 11. **Purchase Power of the U.S. Dollar During the Era of the Federal Reserve**

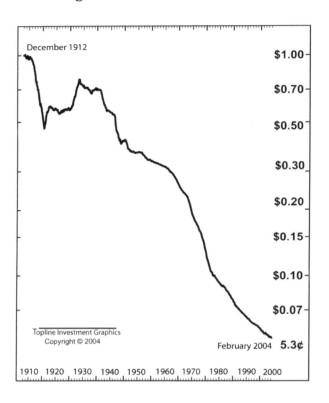

The Dollar Losing Value

As you can see by Dr. Witteveen's comment, made in the mid-1990s, elements in the international community are not favorably disposed to the dollar's centerpiece role in the international monetary system. Such sentiments served as a precursor to major changes in the international financial system only a few years later, when Europe launched its common currency in 1999, not only as an internal mechanism, but as a replacement and competitor to the dollar as a reserve currency. The mere presence of the euro as a viable competitor to the dollar has radically changed the future prospects for the

G is for…

international monetary system as nation-states around the world have slowly, but consistently, began adding it to their reserves.

To be sure, the dollar had already lost 79 percent of its purchasing power since 1970 due to the long-term inflationary policies of the U.S. government and the Federal Reserve (Figure 11). When the inflation trend is coupled with the United States having become the largest debtor nation on earth, these rumblings from the gathering storm clouds, and their potential repercussions, sound ominous indeed. You would be hard pressed to find a country in the world today that would have the wherewithal, or even the desire, to bail out the United States the way this country bailed out Mexico in 1995. On the contrary, most other nations would be scrambling to protect themselves in what could develop into a worldwide economic crash. American investors, in such a

Figure 12. **Federal Budget Surplus or Deficit**

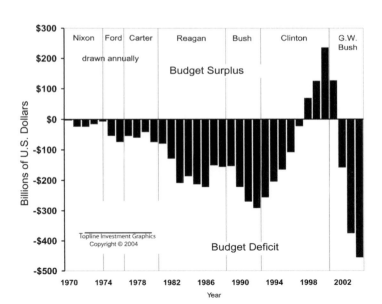

scenario, would be left to their own devices, using whatever means could be found to protect rapidly disintegrating personal asset structures.

The Deficit's Effects on the Economy

We in the United States should take heed of Andrew Tyler's warning—the problems with public debt could very well lead to consequences as destructive as he predicts. In 1945, the national debt stood at $260 billion, a figure few fretted about because we had just fought a war. Government-procured debt is generally considered a consequence of war, and in the first five years after the war, some of the debt was paid down. This, however, was only a brief interlude. Beginning in 1960 and stretching through 2004, there has not been a single year when the national debt has been reduced, not even by a small amount. On the contrary, from Richard Nixon's presidency forward, the smallest annual growth rate in the debt was 3.8 percent in 1974. The largest was a whopping 20.6 percent in 1983, the third year of Ronald Reagan's presidency. In 1970, the accumulated national debt equaled roughly one-third of the gross domestic product. By 2003, it equaled nearly 70 percent—a virtually unsustainable progression.

The federal government deficit figures, which occasionally do show a surplus (Figure 12), do not reflect the real additions to the national debt; instead, they reflect receipts minus expenditures, with borrowings from the Social Security trust fund counted as revenue. As such, the deficit has become more of a political number than one based on sound accounting methods. Nevertheless, a quick review of the numbers from the Nixon era forward is worth the exercise, if only to show how political and economic decision-making affects the numbers.

During the Nixon era, the largest deficit was roughly $60 billion, and that occurred during the prolonged Vietnam War. The deficit spiked during the Gerald Ford years due to a fairly strong recession that encouraged increased government spending. The Jimmy Carter years were relatively subdued from a deficit point of view, even though the nation was crippled by high oil prices and inflation. Under Ronald Reagan, deficits seemingly ran out of control, due primarily to the military buildup that finally brought the Soviet Union to its knees and ended the Cold War. George H.W. Bush's administration inherited the last vestiges of the military buildup under Reagan, including the first Iraq War, and suffered a drop in revenue in the early 1990s recession. The government went into surplus during the Bill Clinton years under the stewardship of Treasury Secretary Robert Rubin and his so-called strong dollar policy. However, under George W. Bush's administration, the United States reels under the high-cost war against terrorism, another recession, and a second, very costly war in Iraq. In fiscal year 2003, the Bush administration added over $550 billion to the national debt in a single year—this is a record. In early 2004, the national debt went over $7 trillion and, if this spending growth rate continues, the Bush administration could very well suffer the indignity of overseeing the first $1 trillion addition to the national debt in a single year.

And if that were not bad enough, the accumulated debt figure we hear so much about does not include the massive spending and obligations that have occurred off budget. CNNMoney recently reported that Jagadeesh Gokhale, an economist with the Cleveland Federal Reserve and the American Enterprise Institute (AEI), and Kent Smetters, an economist at the Wharton School, project a $44 trillion shortfall between revenue and future obligations, fueled primarily by Social Security and Medicare payments and expected to mushroom when the Baby Boom generation begins to reach retirement age.

The net interest on the U.S. national debt approximates 17 percent of what the government collects in individual and corporate taxes. Interest payments, even with rates at lows not seen since the 1960s, are still the third largest federal government expenditure, after military defense and social welfare spending. This begs the question, "What would happen if interest rates moved up by even one or two percent?" Perhaps the economic planners in Washington D.C. do not want to know. Perhaps *we* do not want to know. It may be too frightening a scenario. The national debt, like Frankenstein's monster, has taken on a life of its own.

Most have heard about the debt clock ticking upward at the rate of roughly $2 billion per day, approaching at the current rate over $700 billion per year. But few understand what these numbers mean to the average American. The current national debt translates to $24,000 for every man, woman, and child in the United States, or nearly $100,000 for the typical American family of four. That debt load increases by roughly $5,000 annually, with no end in sight.

Debt's Impact on American Investors

The impact of the national debt on each American citizen cannot be fully understood unless we first understand how it affects the dollar. To put the correlation as simply as possible: As the debt rises, it drives down the purchasing power of the dollar. Inflation, despite political rhetoric to the contrary, has become a way of life in this country. Since 1970, the consumer price index has risen 491.5 percent and, if the dollar were to lose its advantage as the world's reserve currency, the inflation problem could escalate beyond limits tolerable to most Americans.

These facts concerning the value of the dollar—more than any economic treatise, more than any documentary, more than any politician's speech—tell the story of what has happened to the United States. It tells why we work five months of the year to pay our taxes; why the national savings rate is one of the worst in the Western world; why inflation is endemic in our society despite claims that it is dead; why we can't seem to get ahead despite our best-laid plans and hard work. As the dollar has deteriorated, so has the American lifestyle. Unfortunately, it appears this set of circumstances will not likely be reversed anytime soon. The government simply soaks up too much capital—too many tax dollars and too much of the available lending pool.

G is for...

Government economists used to tell us that the national debt doesn't matter because we owe it to ourselves. Although a specious argument, even that rationalization is no longer true. The United States is now the largest debtor nation on earth. No country runs even a close second. We no longer simply owe the national debt to ourselves. In fiscal year 2003, foreign-held U.S. Treasury debt had expanded $260 billion over the previous twelve months—an astonishing surge of over 20 percent—and much of it went into foreign central banks.

Although most in the international investment community deem a default on the U.S. debt unthinkable, default remains one of only three methods of eliminating debt (paying it or inflating it away being the other two), and it cannot be ruled out entirely. Default, needless to say, does have severe consequences for the individual holding that debt as an asset on the balance sheet, either outright or in the form of money market deposits.

As an example, *Financial Times* recently ran an article on Argentina's debt default and the impact on the average Argentinean pensioner, who bought government bonds based on their belief that it would be a solid risk. In late 2001, Argentina defaulted on about $100 billion of its sovereign debt, including that held by its own citizens. The article tells the story of a 68-year-old Argentinean citizen who since has not seen a centavo of his money. "I worked my entire life," he says, "lent the state money when it needed it, and I was punished for it. Having to rely on my family makes me feel worse than useless." Says another retiree who lost his savings in the debacle: "We [Argentineans] are set to suffer more than anyone because, unlike foreign investors, we have a government that does not listen to us or defend us." The government is locked in high-profile negotiations with its international creditors to restructure the debt, but as *Financial Times* points out, the best outcome for the private saver will likely be that "they would see their savings cut in half."

Although default remains a potentiality for the U.S. national debt, the more likely scenario would be the other track, inflating the debt away. Dollar depreciation appears a much more palatable alternative to America's overseas creditors: a slow dwindling away of the dollar as the world's chief reserve currency and a long-term policy of dollar depreciation, over the chasm of default. And that alternative inevitably will lead to consequences of its own.

Debt Monetization: The Road to Inflation

In 2003, amidst the rising spectre of deflation, Federal Reserve Board member Benjamin Bernanke caused quite a stir in financial circles with his observation:

> Like gold, U.S. dollars have value only to the extent that they are strictly limited in supply. But the U.S. government has a technology, called a printing press (or, today, its electronic equivalent), that allows it to produce as many U.S. dollars as it wishes at essentially no cost. By increasing the number of U.S. dollars in circulation, or even by credibly threatening to do so, the U.S. government can also reduce the value of a dollar in terms of goods and services, which is equivalent to raising the prices in dollars of those goods and services. We conclude that, under a paper-money system, a determined government can always generate higher spending and hence positive inflation . . .

With that statement, Bernanke let the cat out of the bag. The ways of Washington and the Federal Reserve could be even more profligate if need be, so let's not concern ourselves with something as loathsome as a deflation. When Bernanke alluded to the "printing press...or its electronic equivalent," he was referring to the process of monetization.

Monetization and the inner sanctum of government finance are quite often written about in such arcane, highly specialized language that few—including other economists—understand what the writer is trying to convey. In simple terms, *monetization* amounts to nothing more than printing money. It works like this: When the federal government cannot find domestic or foreign buyers for its debt issue (usually because the interest rate is not high enough to attract lenders—a problem particularly acute in a low-interest-rate environment), the Federal Reserve Bank buys this debt and issues a check to the government. The government spends this money and in turn debases all the currency outstanding.

This is a sophistication of a process first utilized by the Roman emperors. They would take Roman aureus into the treasury as tax payments, shave some gold off the edges, remelt the shavings and mint them into more coins. The debased coins and the new coins would then be recirculated as equivalent in value. The quantity of gold in circulation was not increased, only the number of aureii. Since an increasing supply of aureii was chasing roughly the same amount of goods, the net result was one of the first forms of currency inflation.

The modern Federal Reserve engages itself in much the same process when it monetizes debt. The most likely times for inflationary outbursts are the 18 to 24 months following a presidential election. Federal Reserve chairmen, whether named by Republican or Democratic administrations, have a tendency to monetize more debt previous to a presidential election in order to keep interest rates down and the economy moving in the right direction. A rising inflation rate in the ensuing years is the direct cost. The greatest inflations have been those following elections. The 1973–1974 outburst followed the 1972 election year. The 1977–1979 outburst followed the 1976 election. Even during the disinflationary 1980s, the inflation rate jumped proportionately following the 1984 and 1988 elections.

In 1992, a record $38 billion was monetized by the Federal Reserve, belying claims by some political pundits that George H.W. Bush lost because the Fed failed to accommodate his reelection. By way of comparison, $14 billion was monetized in 1990 and $24 billion in 1991. Needless to say, in the months before the 2004 election, the Fed went out of its way to accommodate the goal of getting George W. Bush reelected, and it remains to be seen what that accommodation might produce in terms of inflation from 2005 onward. In the spring of 2004, before the electioneering had even begun, American consumers were already being subjected to record gasoline prices among other manifestations of inflation.

In addition to the efforts of the Fed to stimulate the economy, another additional inflationary engine is at work that, at this time, only a handful of analysts have begun to unravel. That is the process of indirect monetization now occurring in the United States through government bond purchases by exporting nation-states like Japan and China. Covered more thoroughly in Chapter 20, this is an even more deadly and virulent form of inflation because the Federal Reserve has lost control of the money-printing process.

This means that how much inflation will be created in the United States is now heavily influenced by China, Japan, and other exporting nations, and they have their own interests in mind, not those of the United States. No one knows how this might all settle out in the American economy, but let's just say the task before Fed chairman Alan Greenspan is far different and far more threatening than anything faced by previous Fed chairmen. The United States may no longer be in control of its own monetary policy, and that is a frightening proposition, to say the least. Already commodity prices are rising strongly—an indication perhaps of what's ahead, not just for the American economy but economies around the world.

The Politics of Debt

Again, building on Alexander Tyler's famous quote, the American political process today is characterized by the politics of debt, in which one group having claims on the government treasury contends with another group with claims of its own. The American people, who underwrite this debt, are essentially unrepresented in the process. This fact lies at the heart of discontent in the United States today. The political parties—the Democrats, who essentially represent the entitlement receivers, and the Republicans, who represent the subsidy-receiving major corporations—have lost all semblance of the ideals upon which the nation was founded.

Taylor Caldwell, in her book *Lion of God* on the life of Paul of Tarsus, echoes Tyler's observation:

> [Rome's] constitution was inevitably eroded by ambitious and wicked and lustful men, in whom patriotism had long died, and who saw their nation not as a Colossus of freedom in the world and a light to the nations, but an arena in which they could gain prizes and eventually crown themselves.

Few can read either Tyler's or Caldwell's words without thinking about what goes on in modern-day Washington D.C. Government debt and all that it represents will remain one of the primary, if not *the* primary motivation for gold ownership.

8

H is for...
The History of Gold since 1971

History is philosophy learned from examples.
—Thucydides

Mark Twain once said that "history does not repeat, it rhymes." For the student of financial markets, gold's history offers a prism through which one can gain a more thorough understanding of the contemporary economy. It also lays the groundwork for the investor hoping to make an educated guess how the *past* might very well rhyme with the *future.*

The most significant events in the modern history of gold are the Gold Standard Act of 1900, by which the United States joined most of Europe in a gold-based economic system; the Federal Reserve Act of 1913, by which the United States entered upon the long road to severing the dollar's link to gold; Franklin Delano Roosevelt's devaluation of the dollar in the 1930s and the subsequent confiscation of gold; the Bretton Woods Agreement following World War II, which fixed the dollar to gold and the rest of the world's currencies to the dollar; and finally the *abandonment* of Bretton Woods and the further devaluation of the dollar during Richard Nixon's presidency in the early 1970s.

Modern Economic Era

For our purposes, the modern economic era began in 1971. That year, President Richard Nixon abandoned the Bretton Woods Agreement, devalued the dollar, raised the fixed price of gold fictitiously to $37.50, and slammed shut the gold window to stop an international run on the U.S. gold reserve. Previous to Nixon's actions, the United States had reduced its once prodigious gold hoard of over 20,000 tonnes to just a little over 8,000 tonnes in an effort to support the $35 international benchmark. Much of the U.S. hoard went overseas, particularly to Europe. Two years later, the U.S. government raised its fixed gold price to $42.22. The dollar was freed to float against the rest of the world's currencies. Gold began to trade freely in gold markets around the world. Nixon's actions also gave a green light to uninhibited budget and trade deficits.

The United States is no longer required to deliver gold to any nation that steps up to the gold window and demands gold for dollars. In subsequent years, this would become the political equivalent to a license to inflate—something this country subscribes to with a vengeance. To this day, the U.S. gold reserve of roughly 260 million ounces ostensibly is valued at $42.22 per ounce, despite the fact that the free market price is closer to $400. At the time, Richard Nixon proclaimed, "We are all Keynesians." This was his way of saying that the forces of sound money were no longer to be represented in American politics, not even by the hard money and conservatively inclined Republican Party. The abrogation of the Bretton Woods Agreement—the international economic structure based on gold that had been in place since World War II—laid the foundation for the modern private gold market. When politicians took gold out of the national money, which is what Nixon did, the need for private gold ownership was enhanced as a means to protect wealth.

By 1973, gold climbed to $120 as price inflation gripped the nation. In that year, the federal debt stood at $466 billion, small by today's standards and representing only 34 percent of the gross domestic product. Double-digit inflation plagued the American economy in 1974. The stock market corrected significantly. That year Richard Nixon resigned from office under the pale of the Watergate scandal. The gold price hit $200, 5.5 times the price targeted in the late 1960s as gold's benchmark.

Carter Administration

The recession years of 1975 and 1976 saw gold in a downtrend, bottoming out at $104. Jimmy Carter was elected president. Continued loose monetary policies, deficit spending, and an embargo against the United States by the Organization of Petroleum Exporting Countries (OPEC) exacerbated an already fragile international monetary situation. Inflation dominated the financial scene. The International Monetary Fund (IMF) and the United States launched monthly gold auctions in 1975. Publicly, the government announced that the sales were intended to meet the newly generated demand resulting from the legalization of private gold ownership in the United States. The real reasons for the sales were to demonetize gold once and for all and to keep the price below $150. Nearly 1,200 tonnes of metal were expended by the IMF and the U.S. Treasury to no avail. By 1977, the price broke out again. In 1978, it was trading in the $250 range. Since U.S. Treasury and IMF sales were having no effect on the gold price, the sales were curtailed in 1978. Gold went through the roof, making progress toward its all-time high. By 1979, the nation and the world had become engulfed in a full-blown monetary crisis. Gold peaked at $875 in a buying frenzy.

Reagan Administration

Ronald Reagan, vowing to bring stability to a troubled nation, was elected president in 1980, unseating the incumbent Jimmy Carter. Interest rates hit 19 percent, an unheard-of level, but this cooled the gold market and brought some stability to the dollar. Gold prices bottomed at just under $300 in 1982, but in 1983, in what turned out to be a minor currency crisis in Europe resulting from the stronger dollar, gold investment demand drove the price back up to $500. Also in 1983, the United States posted its highest unemployment rate since 1941.

The American economy had entered an era of high interest rates, high unemployment, and a subdued, yet still high inflation rate. This combination of factors came to be known as *disinflation*. These circumstances dominated the financial markets as well, and the groundwork was laid for the long-term bull market in stocks and the dollar. A combination of high real interest rates (yields minus the inflation rate) and an abundance of oil kept the inflation rate in check and the gold price from rising radically. The national debt went over $2 trillion, a disturbing benchmark at the time. Seventy banks failed in 1987 alone, the most since the Great Depression, and the United States became the greatest debtor nation on earth. The stock market crashed, and gold shot back up to $500. The world's central banks, in concert with the mining companies, began another assault on gold through their gold lending and carry-trade schemes, quickly driving gold back down to the $350 level.

George H.W. Bush Administration
George H.W. Bush became president in 1988 and was immediately greeted by the worst banking crisis in U.S. history. In what came to be known as the S&L crisis, $300 billion was committed to bailing out mismanaged and sometimes fraudulently run savings and loan institutions. The national debt went over the $3 trillion mark, just three years after breaking the $2 trillion figure. By 1990, the economy was again in recession. For the first time since 1980, the United States posted a negative growth number for the gross domestic product. The Soviet Union broke up, forever altering the international political landscape. Germany reunified. The United States subdued Saddam Hussein and Iraq in the (first) Gulf War, the highlight of George H.W. Bush's presidency. The Cold War ended.

In the United States, massive back-to-back deficits pushed the accumulated federal debt over $4 trillion, just two years after breaking the $3 trillion mark. In 1992, the United

States ran its biggest deficit in history—$290 billion. Gold remained in the doldrums under the influence of continuing official sales and continued forward selling from the mining companies.

Clinton Administration

Gold was driven back down, bottoming at $330, as Bill Clinton was inaugurated President. Pushed by a Japanese banking crisis, a monetary crisis in Europe, and the belief that Bill Clinton's administration would rekindle an inflationary economy, resurgent gold demand drove the price back up to the $425 level. Gold production began to fall, while demand for gold reached record levels worldwide, particularly in the Far East. Only record forward sales by the mines and official central bank sales (detailed in Chapter 6) kept the price from bolting higher. In 1995, the United States, mired in economic problems of its own, bailed out Mexico. The federal government shut down during a budget battle between the Republican-controlled U.S. Congress and the Democratic Clinton administration. Gold began to rise in early 1996, once again challenging the $425 mark. The national debt went past $5 trillion, a figure representing over 70 percent of the gross domestic product. As 1996 drew to a close, gold returned to the $370 level under pressure from heavy forward sales by South African mining companies. Alan Greenspan warned of "irrational exuberance" in the financial markets.

Early 1997 saw the Dow Jones Industrial Average (DJIA) reach a record high. The gold price remained relatively flat for most of the year, held down by central bank sales from the Netherlands, Australia, and Argentina. A study group in Switzerland recommended a phased sale of 1,400 tonnes from the Swiss national reserve. An Asian currency crisis took hold and spread from nation to nation in the Pacific Rim, wreaking havoc in one economy after another. By the end of the year, the Dow had begun to fall rapidly, signaling the end of the long bull market in stocks and vindicating Alan Greenspan's earlier warning about "irrational exuberance" gripping the nation.

The year 1998 began with concerns mounting globally that the Asian Contagion might not be contained. Russia defaulted on its national debt, wreaking havoc with financial institutions globally. Long Term Capital Management, a hedge fund advised by a Nobel Prize laureate, went under and was bailed out by key Wall Street financial firms. Amidst all the uncertainty, gold hit a 19-year low at $270. Concerned that the Contagion could affect the banking system in the industrialized world, the investing public put strong pressure on available gold supplies.

Although the year started quietly, 1999 turned out to be one of the most important and volatile years for gold since the early 1980s. In May, the Bank of England announced it would sell over half of its remaining gold reserve by auction. The gold market went into a tailspin, ratcheting down to $250. Then, in September 1999, the market abruptly moved to nearly $340 per ounce when the 15 top European central banks agreed to cap gold sales and leasing. That announcement pushed a number of bitterly hedged mining companies into financial straits, including Ghana's Ashanti Goldfields and Canada's Cambior Mines. The euro was officially introduced. The year 1999 is generally believed to be a transitional period for gold—the last year of a long gold bear market and the beginning of what many analysts see as a long-term secular bull market. Safe haven gold buyers pushed premiums on pre-1933 U.S. and European gold coins to double previous levels, hedging risks associated the year 2000 (Y2K) computer problems coupled with concerns about the spread of the Asian Contagion to U.S.-based banks.

George W. Bush Administration

In 2000, the stock market's woes continued and investors increasingly began looking around for alternatives, with gold becoming one of the chief beneficiaries. The Dow Jones Industrial Average (DJIA) peaked at over 11,700. On September 11, 2001, hijackers crashed jetliners into the World Trade Center, the Pentagon, and a Pennsylvania field, setting off a new wave of gold buying among international investors concerned about the potential for a long-term war against terror-ism and the effect it might have on the flow of oil from the Middle East.

Then in 2001, gold returned to a low of $250 and there-after began a rally that took it back over the $400 level for the first time since 1993. In both 2002 and 2003, gold appreciated in the 20-percent range. Hedge fund and producer buying un-derpinned the gold market action, and scandals mounted on Wall Street. In 2001, the United States launched a war in Af-ghanistan, and the Second Iraq War was launched in 2003. The United States ran record trade and budget deficits.

It is important for investors to understand that there is more to the gold market than the basic supply and demand tables that characterize other commodities. The story behind the tables—the history of gold—contributes substantially to its ebb and flow on the price charts. Beyond the fundamen-tals, gold is a political metal, and understanding its long his-tory and its role in human affairs adds to an understanding of its place in the overall investment portfolio.

The following annotated graphs (Figures 13 through 17) tell this short history of gold since 1971, for a good start to this understanding. I attempt to summarize the important eco-nomic and political events that have accompanied gold's er-ratically upward climb. Study them well, for gold's history is our own.

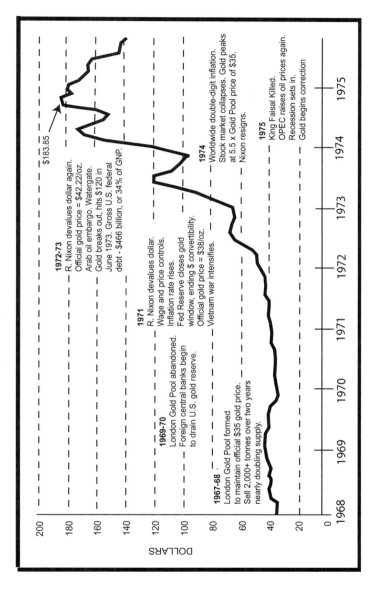

Figure 13. **History of Gold 1968 to 1975**

H is for…

79

Figure 14. **History of Gold 1976 to 1983**

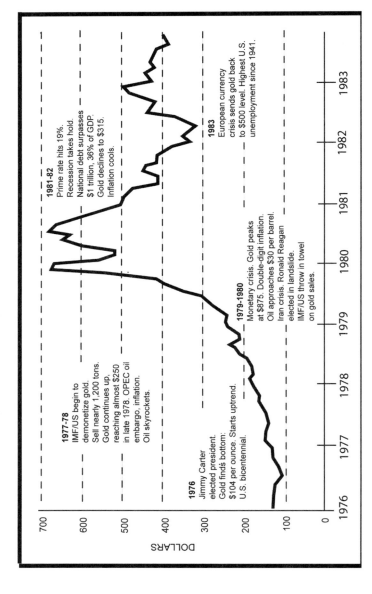

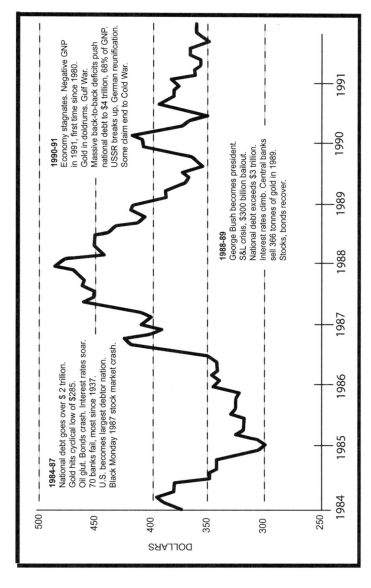

Figure 15. **History of Gold 1984 to 1991**

Figure 16. **History of Gold 1992 to 1996**

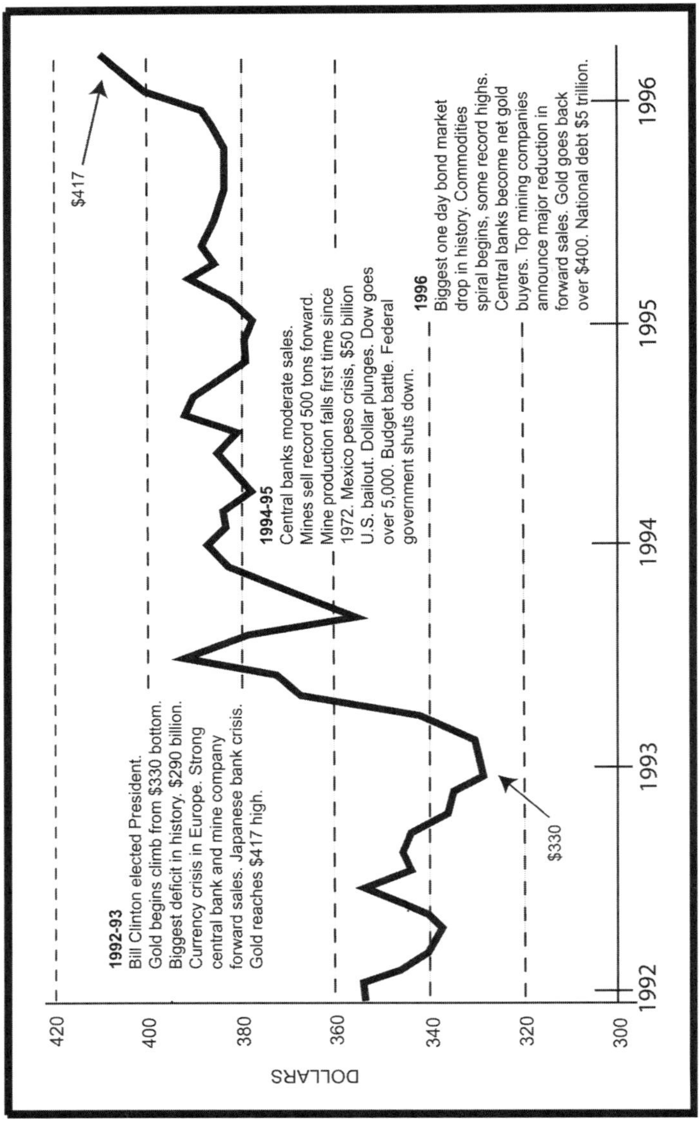

1992-93
Bill Clinton elected President.
Gold begins climb from $330 bottom.
Biggest deficit in history, $290 billion.
Currency crisis in Europe. Strong
central bank and mine company
forward sales. Japanese bank crisis.
Gold reaches $417 high.

1994-95
Central banks moderate sales.
Mines sell record 500 tons forward.
Mine production falls first time since
1972. Mexico peso crisis, $50 billion
U.S. bailout. Dollar plunges. Dow goes
over 5,000. Budget battle. Federal
government shuts down.

1996
Biggest one day bond market
drop in history. Commodities
spiral begins, some record highs.
Central banks become net gold
buyers. Top mining companies
announce major reduction in
forward sales. Gold goes back
over $400. National debt $5 trillion.

$417

$330

DOLLARS

420 400 380 360 340 320 300

1992 1993 1994 1995 1996

Figure 17. **History of Gold 1997 to 2004**

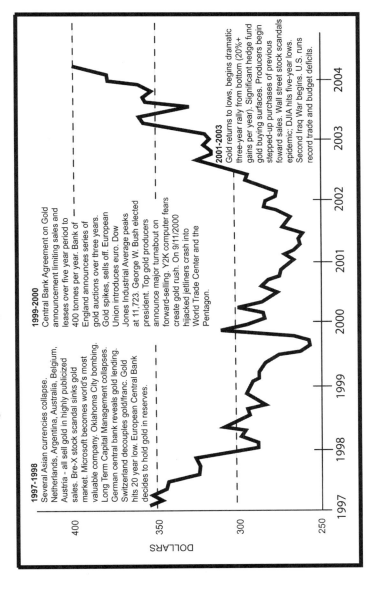

1997-1998
Several Asian currencies collapse.
Netherlands, Argentina, Australia, Belgium, Austria - all gold in highly publicized sales. Bre-X stock scandal sinks gold market. Microsoft becomes world's most valuable company. Oklahoma City bombing. Long Term Capital Management collapses. German central bank reveals gold lending. Switzerland decouples gold/franc. Gold hits 20 year low. European Central Bank decides to hold gold in reserves.

1999-2000
Central Bank Agreement on Gold announcement limiting sales and leases over five year period to 400 tonnes per year. Bank of England announces series of gold auctions over three years. Gold spikes, sells off. European Union introduces euro. Dow Jones Industrial Average peaks at 11,723. George W. Bush elected president. Top gold producers announce major turnabout on forward-selling. Y2K computer fears create gold rush. On 9/11/2000 hijacked jetliners crash into World Trade Center and the Pentagon.

2001-2003
Gold returns to lows, begins dramatic three-year rally from bottom (20%+ gains per year). Significant hedge fund gold buying surfaces. Producers begin stepped-up purchases of previous foward sales. Wall street stock scandals epidemic; DJIA hits five-year lows. Second Iraq War begins. U.S. runs record trade and budget deficits.

DOLLARS

9

I is for…
The Inflation-Deflation Debate:
Either Way, Gold Is a Winner

Nothing wreaks more havoc on the investment portfolio than the two extremes of a monetary policy gone awry, inflation and deflation. Webster defines *inflation* as "an increase in the volume of money and credit relative to available goods and services resulting in a continuing increase in the general price level." It defines *deflation* as the opposite, "a contraction in the volume of available money and credit that results in a general decline in prices." Inflation that has spun out of control is referred to as *hyperinflation*. The most widely cited example of a hyperinflationary breakdown is 1920s Germany. Deflation that has spun out of control is referred to as a *panic* or an economic *depression*. The most cited example of deflationary spiral is the worldwide depression of the 1930s.

Ever since Richard Nixon took the United States (and the world) off the gold standard in 1971, an ongoing debate has been waged between those who believe the American economy is headed for a hyperinflationary spiral and those who believe that a deflationary collapse is inevitable. Volumes have been written espousing both scenarios. Newsletter writers seem to be divided evenly on the subject.

History shows that gold, better than any other asset, protects against both calamities. At some times, like the 1970s, the inflationists appeared to be right. At other times, such as the early 1990s, the deflationists appeared to be right. Thus far we have escaped either extreme. Instead of inflation followed by deflation, we have had inflationary episodes followed by disinflationary or stagflationary episodes wherein the inflation rate has simply been moderated. For example, the inflation rate of his time was enough for Richard Nixon to impose wage and price controls on the economy in 1972. Now it is considered to be a sign that inflation is under control.

There is little doubt that in the present fiat-money-based U.S. economy, launched in 1971, the underlying bias has been inflationary, as shown in other chapters of this book. But this does not mean that the overall inflationary trend will not at some point resolve itself in a deflationary blow-off. In the interim, the nuances and possibilities of either, and their likely effect on the investment portfolio, will remain the subject of a great deal of discussion by laypeople, economists, and financial analysts alike.

The View from Deflationists

Deflationists argue that, with public and private debt at record levels and growing with unrestricted abandon now, the debt can never be sustained or paid off. They say it will be liquidated through default. As bankruptcies mount, banks will fail. Fearful investors will scramble to unload their stocks and bonds. A crash will ensue. In such a scenario, gold becomes the asset of last resort, and possibly the only asset other than cash ($100 bills) worth owning. Some analysts predict gold prices in the thousands of dollars in such scenarios.

The View from Inflationists

Inflationists paint a different picture. The Federal Reserve could be forced to print money (monetize debt) in ever-increasing increments to keep the government in opera-

Figure 18. **Gold in U. S. Dollars, Constant Dollars**

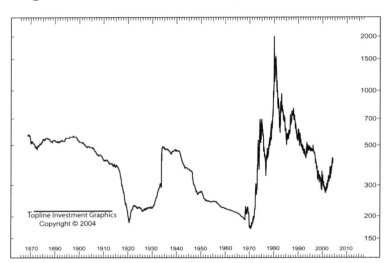

Topline Investment Graphics
Copyright © 2004

tion. This paper blizzard will wend its way through the economy, pushing prices higher and higher. Exporters to the United States, particularly oil exporters, will be forced to continuously ratchet up prices to receive real value for their exported goods. Since oil in particular is the lifeblood of the economy and is a cost component of just about everything we consume, all prices will be pushed higher still. Inflation would then begin to compound itself. The situation could become exacerbated, much as it did in the late 1970s, only this time the inflation flies out of control. Hyperinflation ensues, and gold skyrockets.

Gold's Value

No one knows off which side of the high-wire—hyperinflation or deflationary crash—the economy will fall. Neither proposition is very comforting to the general investor. Yet to the gold investor, the inflation-deflation debate is purely academic. The accompanying chart (Figure 18) shows the purchasing power of gold from the 1870s to present in terms of the price of gold versus consumer prices. As you can see, two economic episodes stand out on the chart, the *deflationary* 1930s and the *inflationary* 1970s. In both anomalies—and gold is owned precisely to weather such anomalies—the value of gold rose dramatically.

In the early 1930s, its purchasing power rose because the prices of goods and services dropped across the board. And in 1933, when President Franklin Roosevelt closed the banks, called in gold bullion, and raised the U.S. benchmark price from $20.67 to $35 per ounce, the purchasing power of gold rose dramatically. Likewise in the 1970s, the gold price rose, outpacing a virulent double-digit inflation rate, thus once again preserving the purchasing power of the gold owner. Sophisticated investors almost always ask how gold performs in both deflationary and inflationary scenarios. Gold, as this important chart demonstrates, will protect and preserve your assets in either instance. Gold is the time-honored, historically proven hedge against economic disasters of all descriptions.

Both deflationists and inflationists recommend gold as the portfolio item to hedge against disaster. In a deflationary crash, gold becomes one of the only assets left standing after all others are destroyed by default. In an inflationary debacle, gold survives the destruction of the currency and retains its value after all other currency-based assets are wiped out. Hedge your portfolio with gold and leave the inflation-deflation argument to the economists.

10

J is for...
Jump-Starting Your Portfolio Plan Through Gold Ownership

The rich old speculator Bernard M. Baruch forehandedly bought gold and gold shares after the 1929 Crash. Years later a suspicious Treasury Secretary asked him why. Because, Baruch replied, he was "commencing to have doubts about the currency." Many are beginning to doubt the strength of the dollar, as they well might. Following Baruch's example, they should lay in some gold as a hedge.
—James Grant, *Grant's Interest Rate Observer*

Essentially, there are two broad categories of gold investors: those who want a safe haven to hedge disaster, and those who simply want to make a profit. A third type of investor seeks to combine both objectives. Your needs will determine what you include in your portfolio. Some thought and attention must be given to which of the three categories you belong. Along these lines, if you place yourself in the hedge disaster category, you must also determine which economic disaster you consider most likely to occur—inflation, deflation, or both. What you decide in this respect will play a determining role in how your portfolio should be structured. Portfolio planning is inherently a very personalized business.

It cannot be done without strong input from the client. Do your homework. Know what you want to accomplish. It is very important to making wise gold investing decisions.

To plan your portfolio properly, consult with a professional in the gold business. Stock brokers, financial planners, mutual fund sales personnel and the like have little knowledge of the highly specialized field of gold coin and gold investing. As a result, they sometimes confuse more than help. Quite often, the course they recommend has more to do with their own interests than what is best for the client.

Safe-Haven Investors

Those oriented toward hedging disaster generally prefer a combination of gold bullion coins and pre-1933 European and U.S. gold coins. The customary split is half of each. The bullion coins will protect your portfolio against currency deterioration, inflation, deflation, bank failures, stock and bond market collapses—the gamut of financial evils. What they won't protect you against is intervention in the gold market by the federal government, including a potential confiscation, or gold call-in, as occurred in the United States in 1933. For an extra layer of protection against government intervention, you will want to include the historically significant pre-1933 European and/or lower-grade uncirculated pre-1933 United States $20 gold coins. Although complete protection cannot be guaranteed through the ownership of pre-1933 gold coins (in the United States, gold ownership is a privilege, not a right), precedent does offer a strong argument in their favor as historically relevant items.

Be prepared to pay marginal premiums over gold coins of contemporary manufacture even though, by and large, these items still track the gold price. If you rate the possibility of confiscation low, then you should weight your portfolio in the direction of bullion coins—anywhere from 60 to 100 percent. If you are concerned about confiscation and other forms of government intervention in the gold market (such as capital controls), you should weight your holdings in the direction of the historic pieces—anywhere from 60 to 100 percent, depending upon your level of concern.

Speculative Investors

Those who approach gold primarily for its profit potential generally stick with the gold bullion coins because of the low premiums, narrow spreads, and ease of liquidity. Thought should be given, however, to the white metals as well—silver, platinum, and palladium—but these are highly specialized markets that must be analyzed separately for their potential. Each is subject to its own set of supply-demand fundamentals. Platinum has a history of outperforming gold in rising markets, and during 2003 and early 2004 it certainly lived up to that billing, trading at nearly $900 as this is written. Keep in mind that silver, platinum, and palladium are primarily inflation hedges. They do not perform well in deflationary economies. Investors whose primary interest is profit should also evaluate the potential in the higher-grade U.S. gold coins, particularly mint state 63, 64, and 65 $20 gold pieces, graded by the independent services. This area is generally recommended for those seeking a higher risk-reward ratio. After years of dormancy, the higher-end collector gold coin market came to life beginning in late 2003, as investors across the country rediscovered this opportunity. If you wish to pursue a speculative approach to gold and the other precious metals, you should decide your portfolio composition under the guidance of an expert who can review with you the merits of each investment.

Combining Safe-Haven and Speculative Investing

If you wish to combine safe-haven and speculative investing, the process becomes a little more complicated. You will need to decide various portfolio weightings. Timing also becomes an issue. You will need some combination of pre-1933 gold coins, gold bullion coins, and/or silver, platinum, and palladium bullion bars to achieve this objective. Additionally, you should review the merits of each investment with a professional advisor, and then determine on your own how your portfolio should be structured, utilizing the guidelines herein as a template.

Miscellaneous Portfolio Concerns

If you think you might need to use gold as money, you should add 1/4-ounce bullion coins and/or pre-1933 European gold pieces that contain approximately ¼ and 1/5 of an ounce of gold. These versatile pre-1933 European gold coins fulfill two functions: utility as a form of money, along with the protection offered by historic items. An alternative or addition would be the $1,000 face value bags of pre-1965 silver coins that contain 715 ounces of silver and trade relatively close to the silver content.

If you wish to hedge both inflation and deflation simultaneously, gold is your best bet. Gold tends to rise as the currency depreciates in inflationary times. In deflationary times, it tends to at least hold its value as the price level drops on most other items, thus preserving the gold owner's purchasing power. At the same time, some analysts argue for much higher gold prices during deflation simply because gold is one of the few investments that would survive a massive debt default and bank panic. Such a scenario would generate unprecedented demand, which would drive prices higher. If you feel inflation is the most likely future scenario, silver and platinum should be added to the mix. Another possibility for inflation hedgers is graded rare coins, which have performed extraordinarily well during past inflationary episodes.

Know Thyself

Defining your particular goals and needs before buying your first ounce of gold is a critical elemental to a successful portfolio approach. With that in mind, a few words are helpful concerning the mind-set with which you pursue your interest in gold ownership.

Some enter the gold market to make a profit, others to hedge disaster, some to accomplish both. No matter into which category you fit, make sure you understand why you are going into the gold market. Convey that understanding to the individual with whom you are structuring your gold portfolio. The whys have quite a bit to do with what you end up owning.

Frequently investors will say that any kind of gold will do because after all gold is gold, isn't it? This type of attitude has helped a great many coin shop owners unload unwanted inventory they hadn't been able to get rid of for years—art bars, commemorative coins, bullion manufactured by little known refiners, and so forth. It has also assisted more than one boiler room operation meet its sales targets, selling exotic gold coins, leveraged precious metals positions, and gold stocks unknown to just about everyone in the industry except the promoter making the offer. This is probably a good deal for the seller, but it could spell disaster for you, the buyer. In the same vein, I have talked to hundreds, probably thousands of investors in over 30 years in the business. Quite often, potential investors have no more reason for buying gold than "everybody else is doing it." Needless to say, if the recent stock market debacle is an example, this is not exactly the best approach to owning any investment, and gold is no exception.

To begin, consider the inscription over the entrance to the temple of the ancient Delphic Oracle: Know Thyself. Know why you want to own gold. Study. Read. Isolate the primary reasons why you have an interest in gold. Contact a few gold firms and ask questions. There's nothing like conversation to stimulate thinking. Take time to lay a little groundwork. Then make your move. The political and economic situation being what it is, there is no better time to start than now. Know thyself—your goals and needs. Be sure that the gold items you buy match those goals and needs, and you will be a more confident, happier gold investor over the long run.

11

K is for...

Kindred Metal—Silver

No discussion of gold investing would be complete without at least a few words about gold's close relative—*silver*. Many associate silver with gold and see it as essentially the same investment—a kindred metal, so to speak—but in reality they are two quite different metals and are used by portfolio planners for two entirely different purposes. The myth that silver is simply poor man's gold is one that has endured over a very long period of time despite the marked differences in the way they have performed under certain economic conditions.

Gold's importance as a portfolio item lies primarily in its monetary value. It is a store of value first and a commodity second, even though it has performed well from a commodity perspective in the past. With silver, the situation is reversed. It is a commodity first and a store of value second. As essentially an industrial metal, it tends to do well in inflationary economies—sometimes phenomenally well—but can severely deflate in a depression.

For these reasons, silver plays an important secondary role in portfolio planning as a way to speculate against the dollar when the inflationary fires are fanned. Silver should not be used as a deflationary hedge for the obvious reason that when the economy and industrial production are weak, so is the demand for silver.

Silver should not be viewed as either a permanent or semipermanent member of the portfolio family. Rather, it should be held for its profit potential and at some point converted back into cash or gold. In past bull markets, even in minibull markets, silver has outperformed gold percentage-wise.

The price history of silver has been substantially more volatile than that of gold, with upsides as well as downsides much more pronounced. A correct call could help you end up with more gold in the long run than if you had purchased only gold to begin with. A bad call will cost you dearly. Be forewarned. By way of illustration, when gold climbed from the $320 level to $430 in 2003–2004, silver went from roughly $4.50 to over $8.00. It then dropped precipitously back to the $5.50 level in a matter of weeks. Gold's downside was much less dramatic, bottoming near $380. As you can see, with silver, timing is everything. You would not have wanted to be one of the investors who bought into the market at $8.00.

Silver is particularly useful to wealthy individuals who have sufficient gold reserves and would now like to branch out into something with stronger profit potential. Silver relies on its market as an industrial commodity for future appreciation. With that in mind, let's briefly review the supply and demand fundamentals.

According to statistics supplied by the Silver Institute, silver production is spread evenly over a large number of countries: Mexico produces roughly 16 percent of the annual supply; Peru, 15 percent; Australia, 10 percent; and China, Poland, Chile, the United States, and Canada all in the 7-percent range. Mine production has risen steadily overall since 1994, when 451 million ounces were produced. In 2003, 595 million ounces were mined. These production figures are likely to continue rising in future years. Silver production is primarily a byproduct of gold and copper mining. If higher prices are in the cards for those metals, then expect silver production to rise. Scrap reprocessing is also an important component of the supply. It has steadily increased over the past ten years as well, from just over 150 million ounces to roughly 190 million ounces in 2003.

For silver to go substantially higher, industrial uses and investment will have to rise enough to outweigh any production increases and, at this time, the uses of silver, including photography, are declining or static at best. Presently the main uses for silver are industrial (39 percent of supply), photography (22 percent), and jewelry/silverware (31 percent). Photographic usage has been static since the mid-1990s at roughly 200 to 220 million ounces. Physical silver sales for investment have waned in recent years, but they will probably pick up if metal prices start rising.

Silver's average price has been steady to down: $5.28 in 1994, $5.22 in 1999, and $4.87 in 2003. Those who buy silver for investment these days do so primarily on the exchanges or options markets. (Hedgers and investors both prefer gold because it is less weighty and cumbersome.) For most investors, silver should be an addendum to the overall portfolio, acquired only after a strong gold position has already been established.

12

L is for...

London, New York, Hong Kong, Zurich: A Day in the Life of the Gold Market

Real gold is not afraid of the fire of a red furnace.
—Chinese proverb

Even as you read this section, a gold price is being posted somewhere in the world. Like the old British Empire, the sun never sets on the gold market (see Figure 19). For centuries, gold has captured the imagination of those with a trading mentality, who dare to buy here and sell there with the hope of making a profit in the bargain. Now with the advent of computer screens, satellite transmissions, and instantaneously e-mailed buy/sell confirmations, the gold market has been internationalized. It is not unusual for a trader in New York to take a position on the London market as he eats breakfast, and then sell that position in Hong Kong or Singapore as he prepares to retire in the evening.

London Market

For American gold traders, the day begins in London. Before traders on the East Coast have had their first cup of coffee, the five members of the London gold market have agreed upon their morning gold fix. They have assessed sup-

Figure 19. **A Day in the Life of the Gold Market**

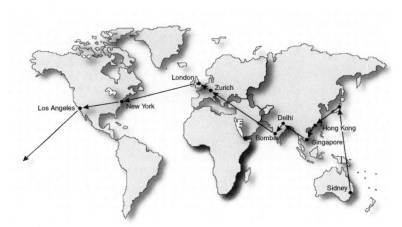

ply and demand for that day. They have also established a price they believe will adequately match the buys and sells streaming in from mining companies, bullion dealers and traders, central banks, internationally-based commercial banks, refiners, and commercial brokerages. If the buys exceed the sells in sufficient quantity, the price is raised. If vice versa, the price is lowered.

In recent years, London has become an increasingly important center for the gold trade, making headway toward its old place at the head of the gold trading table, a place which both COMEX in New York and Zurich have lost. The reasons? London is where the world's central banks and the bullion banks have set up shop for their gold deposit, lending, and derivative operations. London is home to the London Bullion Market Association that trades very high volumes in both physical and paper over-the-counter transactions. Terry Smeeton, who once headed the gold and foreign exchange operations for the Bank of England, estimates that the volume in London is 7.5 million ounces daily. The London market offers both spot and forward sales. Spot sales represent gold sold at the posted London price. Forward sales represent gold sold by contracts in the future at an agreed-upon price, with the London market serving as the go-between.

The five men who set the London fixes represent the largest, oldest, and most influential banks and gold dealers in the world: N.M. Rothschild (which provides the group's chairman), Societe General, the Hong Kong Shanghai Bank (HSBC), Scotia Mocatta, and Deutsche Bank. They set two fixes each day. The first, at 10:30 London time, is known as the A.M. Fix. This is the one usually announced on American radio networks as you commute to work in the morning. The P.M. Fix is set after lunch. The five men meet in the offices of N.M. Rothschild under the watchful eye of the founder himself, Nathan Rothschild, whose portrait hangs appropriately in the conservatively appointed trading room. All business is done under the London Code of Conduct for bullion dealers.

New York Market

The less than polite gold trading pit at the COMEX in New York opens at 8:20 A.M. Eastern Time and begins operations while the London market is still open. The highly charged auction atmosphere of COMEX stands in stark contrast to the restrained, dignified arrangement in London. We have all seen the video clips: frantic traders shouting at each other, waving their arms, pointing fingers, making hand signals—a picture of seeming confusion and anarchy. Interestingly, throughout the apparent chaos runs a thread of perfect order. Buys and sells are actually matched and prices set. Typically, traders in the pit are young men and women for an obvious reason: the frenzy takes its toll. After the terrorist attack of September 11, 2001, which struck at the heart of New York's financial district, the trading day was shortened. The COMEX gold market now closes 1:30 P.M. Eastern Time.

From 1933, when President Franklin D. Roosevelt issued his executive order seizing Americans' gold, until 1975, when President Gerald Ford signed legislation relegalizing it, gold did not trade formally in the United States. With gold's relegalization, interest from the public and the financial community grew rapidly. COMEX moved to meet that interest with its popular 100-ounce futures contract. From the 1970s to present, COMEX became the dominant price-setting market. London challenges that dominance but has yet to supplant it.

COMEX operates on a spacious trading floor in the World Financial Center in downtown Manhattan. The price generated on the trading floor is the one flashed on trading screens across the United States and around the world, and used by gold firms as a base for pricing bullion and bullion coins. With the advent of the Internet, those prices are available by subscription in either real or delayed time, to which most brokers and traders refer continuously during the business day. "COMEX price" and "New York price" are terms often used interchangeably by many gold firms. After COMEX closes, after-hours futures trading is conducted via the NYMEX ACCESS Internet-based trading platform. ACCESS trading begins at 3:15 P.M. Eastern Time, Monday through Thursday, and concludes at 8:00 A.M. the following day. Trading starts for the week on Sunday at 7:00 P.M.

Hong Kong Market

The next big market to trade is Hong Kong, and its pricing is reflected in the ACCESS quotes. The Hong Kong market is venerable in itself, having first traded gold in 1910, when British banks thought they might need a mechanism for trading gold in the Orient. Today it is the launch site for gold going to mainland China, one of the fastest-growing gold markets in the world. In fact, the whole Asian market has been so active in recent years that American and European gold traders who travel there talk about it in the wistful tones normally reserved for the American market of the late 1970s and early 1980s. This market is highly influential in Asia, because Hong Kong is where Japanese investors, banks, and financial houses occasionally hedge their orders and make their physical purchases. It is also in a time zone that fits nicely with the business day of traders in Saudi Arabia and the rest of the Persian Gulf, particularly the new and rapidly growing market in Dubai.

If Hong Kong gold is moving, it is quite often due to buying or selling of the Middle East investors. Large amounts of Hong Kong gold are also made into jewelry for export throughout Asia. For the most part, Hong Kong serves as a convenient midpoint in the trading day because it fills the gap between markets in the United States and Europe.

In *World of Gold*, gold historian and analyst Timothy Green characterizes the Hong Kong market this way:

> They [the Hong Kong traders] like awkward tael-weight bars [based on 1.2-ounce units] and resist suggestions that they should trade in ounces and U.S. dollars to conform to world patterns. They delayed for years the introduction of the Reuters monitor computer system, fearing a computer must invade the secrecy of their 'society.'

For many American and European gold owners, these sentiments do not sound foreign at all.

Zurich Market

The next market to open in gold's day is Zurich, Switzerland. This market is dominated by the big Swiss commercial banks. They first made a splash in the world gold market by convincing South Africa that they would be better merchants for its gold than London, particularly since the Swiss banks would themselves be the end buyers instead of acting as intermediaries like the London banks. Then, in the early 1970s, Russia—at the time the second largest producer of gold to South Africa—began to ship its gold to Switzerland. Zurich in this way became the largest dealer of physical gold bullion in the world, shipping to all corners of the globe.

Now, as Timothy Green puts it, "Gold is as much a part of Switzerland as the Alps and skiing." Switzerland appeals to a great many of the world's private sector gold-holders, the super wealthy who keep a significant portion of their assets in gold. Many individuals who do not trust their own governments admire Switzerland for its secrecy laws and its long history of judiciously handling other people's money. As a result, much of the world's privately held gold is stored secretly in Swiss vaults.

The London market opens while Zurich is still trading. It quite often takes its starting cue from Zurich. So goes gold around the world each day. The sun never sets on the gold market.

13

M is for...
Myths and Realities about Gold

Gold has its critics. Yet most of their criticism is ill-founded and amounts to little more than good propaganda for those who fear strong gold demand will divert investor interest from the equities markets and the dollar. You have probably heard or read most of the standard criticisms. Here are concise and complete rebuttals—the last words on the merits of gold.

Myth: Gold is not a good portfolio item because it doesn't pay interest.

Reality: The fact that gold does not pay interest is its greatest strength. If gold were to pay interest, the return on your gold would be dependent on the performance of another individual or institution. This, of course, is the case with paper assets such as bonds, bank-certified deposits, money market accounts, and even stocks. The contractual relationship between the creditor and the debtor can be a paper asset's greatest strength. It can also be its greatest weakness. An additional and often complicating factor is that paper assets are directly affected by the performance of the currency in which they are denominated.

Gold, on the other hand, is a stand-alone investment independent of government largess or the performance of another individual or institution. This is gold's greatest strength. Even though gold does not pay interest directly, it is interesting to note that over any extended period of time the interest rate of currency becomes imputed in the price. During inflationary periods, the appreciation in the price of gold is the greatest, and so is the rise in interest rates. During deflationary periods the gold price tends to stay flat while interest rates plummet. Gold historically seeks a price level that takes into account the inflation rate of currency. This compensates for its noninterest-bearing status.

Myth: In the long run, stocks always outperform gold, therefore there's no reason to own gold.

Reality: Markets cycle. The performance of the stock market has been fundamentally tied to the performance of the dollar over most of the last century, and even though some on Wall Street would like you to believe in never-ending growth and profits, that is simply not the case in reality. Note the chart (Figure 20) that depicts how many ounces of gold it takes to buy the Dow Jones Industrial Average (DJIA); this is both an indicator of future long-term trends and proof of the cyclic nature of the gold and stock markets. As you can see, well-defined peaks where the Dow-gold relationship favored stocks occurred in the late 1920s, the early 1960s, and the late 1990s at approximately 18 ounces, 28 ounces, and 44 ounces, respectively. From each peak, gold dramatically gained purchasing power in the ensuing years as the Dow dropped and the price of gold rose. As the chart indicates, the Dow achieved its most recent peak in the late 1990s at over 11,000.

If the cyclical relationship between the two holds, and there is every reason to believe it will, we can expect gold to gain in Dow purchasing power over the next decade, bottoming somewhere in the area of one to two ounces. At what price level will they cross? Richard Russell, the widely read market analyst and editor of *Dow Theory Letters*, offers the fol-

Figure 20. **Dow Jones Industrial/Gold How Many Ounces of Gold Buys the Dow Jones Industrial Average?**

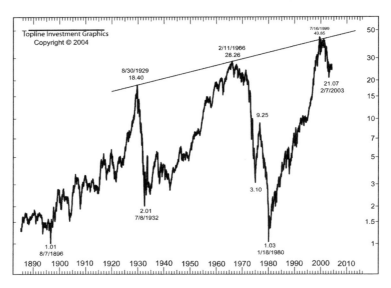

lowing opinion: "My guess is that before the current bull market in gold is over, gold will be priced substantially above the 1980 peak price of $850. How much higher I don't know. At the recent New Orleans seminar I stated that as a guess I believed we'd see the price of the Dow and the price of gold cross. At what level? My guess was around $3,000."

Myth: Gold stocks are a better portfolio option than gold itself.

Reality: Gold stocks are stocks first and gold second. This is an important distinction for investors to recognize, because once it is understood, justifying gold stock ownership as a substitute for gold itself becomes very difficult. Owning gold stocks is not unlike owning other types of stocks. As a matter of fact, in the last three stock market crashes—1929, 1935, and 1987—gold stocks also tumbled into the abyss, belying claims by stockbrokers that they can serve as a disaster hedge and substitute for the metal itself.

In addition, you could presumably own a gold stock during a period of rising gold prices and not participate in the uptrend simply because a company had diminishing prospects in the eyes of the investment community. This is precisely what happened to a large grouping of hedged gold mining companies during the 2002–2003 gold price run-up. They woefully underperformed the gold market amidst cries of foul on the part of a large number of gold stock owners. These companies were excluded from the run-up because they had already sold their gold forward at much lower prices than the current market rate. Beyond hedging, many potential value killers could damage a mining concern: environmental cleanup, permitting, engineering problems, and wage disputes (just to name a few) could easily stand in the way of profits. Gold stocks are not an investment in gold, but in gold producers, with all the nuances attendant to owning stock in any venture. For the safe-haven investor, there is no substitute for owning the real thing.

Myth: Gold is just another commodity, like pork bellies.

Reality: Gold trades on the commodities exchanges along with pork bellies and the other commodities, but here the similarity ends. Unlike other commodities, which are produced primarily for consumption, gold alone is accumulated and saved. It is also the only commodity used as money to facilitate future consumption. Most of the gold ever produced still exists today in one form or another. You cannot say the same thing about pork bellies, soybeans, or sugar. The gold you might someday purchase could very well have been part of the treasury of Rome, or used by Marco Polo in his first visit to China, or circulated as currency in the Old West. This money function, called asset preservation of gold, separates it from the commodity complex and gives it a special place at the very top of the value scale. Those who relegate gold to the status of "just another commodity" usually do so because they either fear gold or do not like competing against it. By denigrating it, they hope to subdue public accumulation—an exercise in futility. Gold is the enduring commodity.

Myth: Gold is a barbarous relic of past monetary systems, irrelevant in today's fast-moving, computerized markets.

Reality: Gold is held as a reserve asset in nearly every central bank in the world. It serves as an asset of last resort to be used for grave international crises such as war, economic calamity, environmental and weather disasters, and the like. Former U.S. Federal Reserve Chairman Paul Volcker made these comments about gold and central banking in answer to the barbarous relic claim:

> We sometimes forget that central banking as we know it today is, in fact, largely an invention of the past hundred years or so, even though a few central banks can trace their ancestry back to the early nineteenth century or before. It is a sobering fact that the prominence of central banks in this century has coincided with a general tendency toward more inflation, not less. By and large, if the overriding objective is price stability, we did better with the nineteenth century gold standard and passive central banks, with currency boards, or even with "free banking." The truly unique power of a central bank, after all, is the power to create money, and ultimately the power to create is the power to destroy.

Other central bankers, including current U.S. Federal Reserve Chairman Alan Greenspan, have voiced similar admiration for this barbarous relic. In lieu of an international gold standard, individual investors have been forced to place themselves on the gold standard even in today's computerized markets. Gold today has the same relevance it has always enjoyed. It is the asset of last resort and has universal value for both individual investors and nation-states.

Myth: World governments in conjunction with the central banks control the gold price. They intend to hold that price down.

Reality: In each instance in modern monetary history, when governments and central banks (including our own federal government and central bank) acted to hold the gold price down, the price was on the verge of moving substantially higher due to the inflationary policies these very same institutions were encouraging. Their activities to hold gold down amounted to exercises in futility, only delaying the dominant, underlying trend. As a matter of fact, government interventions in the gold market in the past (most recently in the 1960s and 1970s) have amounted to no less than solid indicators that the price was about to go substantially higher. Far from being able to control gold, to the consternation of some central bankers and governments, they too must answer ultimately to what the gold market is telling them. When it comes to currency value, gold is the master of all and the slave of none.

Myth: Gold is a speculative, volatile investment that should be avoided by conservative investors.

Reality: It is not gold that changes in value but currencies. What you could purchase with an ounce of gold a hundred years ago, you can purchase with an ounce of gold today. The reason for the spikes dominating the gold charts over the long cycle is not gold's volatility, but rather government and/or central bank intervention to suppress the price. Once market forces overcame the intervention, gold sought its natural price level, which proved to be multiples of the interventionists' target range. Hence the spikes. If the interventionists had not acted to keep the price of gold down, the chart would have a more gradual rise, and gold's critics would be unable to make claims of its volatility.

Myth: Gold is an unpatriotic investment.

Reality: It has become a small world. Investors now invest their money in economies all over the world. Is it unpatriotic for an investor to buy Swiss annuities, or a Japanese equities fund, or a South African gold fund? Would these choices be considered un-American? Probably not. More likely, they would be considered prudent diversifications. There is also the question of whether citizens are obligated to lose their hard-earned wealth holding a currency that is being systematically debased by misguided monetary authorities. As shown in other sections of this book, the monetary policies of the United States virtually assure further devaluation of the dollar in the future.

Far from being unpatriotic, citizens who accumulate gold may be the exact opposite. These citizens could very well turn out to be the country's most farsighted, devoted, and patriotic resource.

Indeed, the fact that certain citizens have the wisdom to accumulate gold may someday be this country's saving grace. If the dollar were to fail, the gold accumulated in the United States by American citizens would become the capital base required for this nation to recover—a thought worth pondering as we close this section.

14

N is for…

Numismatics:
A Diversification Within a Diversification

Numismatics is the study and collection of old and rare coins. In modern times, collecting coins has evolved beyond the simple accumulation of old and interesting coins. It has become a sophisticated investment vehicle and hedge replete with a large number of participants, independent third-party item grading, widely circulated and updated price sheets, large-volume electronic trading, and high-volume purchases and sales. Numismatics has become a popular attraction among well-heeled investors, much like collecting fine oil paintings, gemstones, and antiques. It is not unusual to hear of individual rare coins selling for prices in the seven figures, but the bulk of items are attainable at affordable prices for many investors, and this is the area that receives the most market action.

Numismatics is not for every investor. The bull markets can be incredibly lucrative. The bear markets can be devastating. No investor should acquire truly rare coins as an ultimate hedge against disaster simply because they might be difficult to liquidate in an emergency. As a capital gains vehicle, however, they can be very rewarding. If you can accept the volatile nature of the market as both its greatest detriment and its greatest attribute, then perhaps investing in rare coins is something you should pursue. Be sure you find an experienced adviser. This is not the type of thing most investors can do on their own. Those who try usually regret not having gone with an expert who can act as your ally and confidant in this tricky market.

Building a Portfolio

Investors looking to protect themselves against economic disasters should first build a foundation of gold bullion coins and/or pre-1933 European and U.S. gold coins. Once that foundation is complete, adding rare coins to your portfolio as a growth vehicle is warranted. Rare coins historically have participated in major precious metals rallies, especially if the rallies were inflation-induced. In Germany during the 1920s, when hyperinflation destroyed the mark, substantial assets were saved—and profits won—by investments in numismatics.

Rare coins are generally considered, at minimum, a three-to-five-year investment, although many with a more speculative bent have a shortened time perspective. The market tends to move in fits and starts. Steady appreciation is as rare as the coins in which you are investing. On the other hand, in the long run, coins have an impressive record and historically behave in a way very similar to the stock market. If you go into it with the attitude that you are in the investment for the long run, you will probably do just fine. Of course, there are no guarantees. On the other hand, if you do not have the financial and psychological staying power, the market could teach you one of those lessons you'll wish you never learned.

The rare coin market consists of sectors, much like the stock market. There are silver dollars, small-denomination gold coins, nineteenth-century coins, twentieth-century coins, commemorative coins, and a long list of similar groupings. Like stocks, these sectors tend to attract and repel interest. A sector can sit dormant for years before moving in either direction. Once it starts moving, the action can be fast and furious.

Quite often a sector can double in a single year and then go into dormancy again, or even go down just as rapidly. This market is not for the faint-hearted. If you go into the investment realizing that the holding period is at least three to five years, you stand a good chance of being in the market when it does spike. You might not see any appreciation for the first two years. You might then experience a doubling in the third year, for example, which makes for a nice profit. Patience and tenacity are the keys to success.

Grade and Population of Gold Coins
Grade

Two other factors figure greatly in the success of a numismatic investment: grade and population. *Grade* refers to the quality of the coin. The grading system for investment-grade numismatic items—those disassociated from the bullion value—starts with mint state 64 and proof 64 coins and goes to mint state 70. Very few if any coins are available in the mint state 70 designation. Do not purchase coins below mint state 64 unless the item is a recognized rare date and mint mark. It is better to own one scarce or rare mint state 65, 66, or 67 coin in a series than a dozen mint state 63 coins in the same series.

Many large marketing organizations in the field push low-grade (mint state 63 or less) coins as numismatic investments. But the pros in the field consider these items common, not worthy of the appellation "investment." As a result, when the investment houses are out of the market, which happens frequently, these items are severely discounted. The investor bears the brunt of the devaluation. Scarce and rare coins, on the other hand, enjoy the benefit of a large commonsense market. In this market, the greater the rarity, the better the value in the long run. Any comparative review of price histories in any sector of the coin market bears out this observation.

Note: None of the foregoing analysis applies to $20 gold pieces, which constitute a separate market entirely and must be treated differently. When purchasing rare coins, make sure they have been graded by either the Numismatic Guaranty Corporation (NG) or the Professional Coin Grading Service (PCGS) and are housed in hard plastic containers. This increases their liquidity and narrows the spread between the buy and sell.

Population

Population is the other key factor in numismatic investments. This refers to the number of coins given a specific grade by the grading services. When purchasing rare coins, check their relative rarity, or population figure, against other items in the series or sector. Both grading services publish population reports, which provide this data. Stick with strong, relative rarity or scarcity. It pays in the long run and increases the likelihood that your purchase will be among the beneficiaries if there is a run-up in value for that series.

A couple of additional advantages of coin investing are worth mentioning. There are no reporting requirements for buying or selling, so your privacy is easily maintained. The tax code allows you to trade one numismatic item for another as a "like kind exchange," thus delaying capital gains taxes until you liquidate. As is the case with all tax-related transactions, please check with your tax advisor to make sure your trades qualify for the "like kind" exemption. This allows you to build strong asset value by trading appreciated sectors for sectors that have remained dormant in the hope they will be the next to move upward. Rare coins are excellent wealth builders. A great many investors enter the field of numismatic investing simply for this advantage.

Be aware that the coin market is notoriously thin. It is characterized by both steep run-ups and steep declines. The thin market also creates large spreads between buying and selling when it is in decline and better spreads when it is going up. In a weak market, the selling compounds itself as the coins seek strong hands. In a strong market, it is sometimes (but not always) difficult to find the better items because investors tend to hold out. In numismatics, the byword is patience in both buying and selling. Never allow yourself to feel pressed. If you are forced to sell at the wrong time, you will be at the mercy of the market.

Taken in the right context, coin investing can be both fun and profitable. In the late 1970s and mid-to-late-1980s, the coin market experienced explosive rallies, producing profits three to seven times the base starting point, according to some analysts. So there is no denying the potential. Beginning in 2003, the numismatic market began to show signs of life for the first time in over a decade, and investors quickly returned to this field in search of fun and profit. Before that, the coin market had been in a grinding bear market that began in the early 1990s.

Many rare items can be purchased at a fraction of their late 1980s prices, when the coin market last peaked. Profit-seeking investors might consider a modest commitment while the market is still low. Once again, hedge investors should start with bullion coins and pre-1933 $20 gold pieces and work their way toward numismatics after a foundation is built.

15

O is for...

Options and Futures:
The Tail Wags the Dog

Investors often ask about gold's puzzling, erratic, seemingly inexplicable price behavior. These queries are well justified. Too often, just when you think everything is lined up fundamentally, politically, and economically for gold to make an ascent, it promptly turns on a dime, and performs in a precisely 180-degree fashion. "Why can't gold be more predictable?" goes the familiar refrain. To this, I usually respond, "Where does it say that gold has to be predictable?" The one thing I've learned in over 30 years of watching the gold market is that, just when you become convinced that gold is about to go in one direction or the other, it promptly does the opposite and lets you know who is really the boss.

Options and Futures

The primary reason for this is that the price for gold is not really established in the physical market for gold, but in the options and futures markets, where leveraged (or geared) trading overwhelms the volume in the actual physical market. In this arena, the COMEX gold trading pit or the over-the-counter market in London, the short-term view holds sway over the medium- to long-term. The gold price is determined or discovered not only by the fundamentals, although they play a role, but more directly by the trading activity of thousands of players exercising their commercial or speculative interest.

Overall, this is a more complicated subject than can be properly treated in a general overview like this book. But for the purposes of this chapter, let's concentrate on the activity of one group of important market players who profoundly influence the gold price, the group COMEX calls large speculative traders—a group which claims among its constituents ,massive hedge funds, commodity trading groups, and financial institutions. In my estimation, these groups are capable of moving the gold market in either direction, and hold the key to understanding how the gold price is set on a day-to-day basis.

How the Tail Wags the Dog

Over the years, this process of the gold price being established on the floor of the COMEX instead of the spot market has been characterized as the tail wagging the dog, that is, the paper market "tail" wags the physical market "dog." In turn, none of the players in the COMEX market has more influence on that day-to-day price.mechanism than large-spec traders, the huge capital pools capable of making massive bets on market direction either up or down. In turn, the large spec traders' ability to touch off a cascading herd effect throughout the market has been quantified in several studies of futures market behavior.

An illuminating study by assistant governor to the Reserve Bank of Australia, Bob Rankin, titled *The Impact of Hedge Funds on Financial Markets: Lessons from the Experience of Australia*, frames the impact of these massive capital pools on price discovery:

> Hedge funds have found themselves in a strong position to exploit such trading strategies [re: speculative attacks on national currencies] following their success in the UK devaluation of 1992. The publicity generated by that event gave them

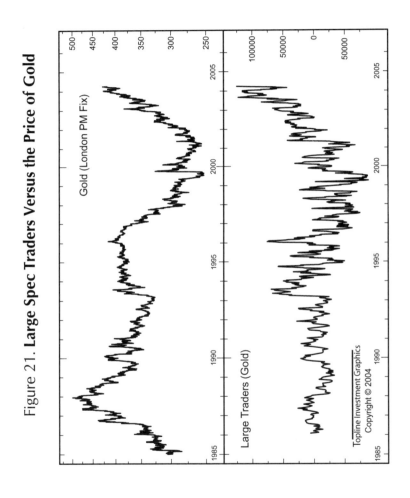

Figure 21. **Large Spec Traders Versus the Price of Gold**

enormous standing in financial markets and many traders adopted strategies that mimicked those of the hedge funds.

In the foreign exchange market in particular, banks and investment banks systematically keep their better clients informed of the hedge funds' daily trading strategies. Combined with the willingness of some hedge funds to use leverage to build very large positions, this status places hedge funds in the position of market leaders, with the ability to influence the behavior of others in markets.

The study concluded that "...the activities of hedge funds came to dominate the market during the middle of the year, affecting the dynamics of price discovery for the period while this dominance continued."

Notice the chart (Figure 21) that shows the nearly direct correlation between large trader speculative positions on the COMEX and the price of gold. Look carefully and you will see that when the large specs are *short* of the market (or sellers), the price tracks down. When they are *long* of the market (or buyers), the price tracks higher. For most of the 1990s, the large-spec volume was on the short side of the market and the price was subdued. But then something very interesting occurred in 1999. Speculative interest, for the first time in over a decade, swung decisively to the long side of the market, and prices in turn were driven dramatically higher, beginning in the early part of the present decade. The question for investors interested in price direction is whether or not those traders are on the long side of the gold market to stay.

Although the COMEX gold trading pit represents only a small part of the overall paper gold trade (the private contract London over-the-counter market dwarfs COMEX volumes), it nevertheless offers a reliable bellwether for the prevailing international sentiment. In fact, in my view, you would be hard pressed to find a stronger, more predictive correlation than the one shown in this simple graph (although always apply the usual caveat that past behavior is not necessarily a guarantor of the future). As such, when viewed in the longer-term perspective represented by this chart, it is evident that indeed a new trend has taken hold in the gold market.

The large speculative interests, probably for the very same reasons spelled out elsewhere in this book (particularly in Chapter 6 on market fundamentals), by and large have become very bullish on gold, as indicated by their persistently growing volume on the long side of the market. In fact, their extraordinary participation on the long side, beginning in December 2002, was the main ingredient in pushing the price to the $400 level—not once, but twice. Again, in 2004 when gold pushed past the $400 level and stubbornly remained at ten-year highs, the move was accompanied by huge participation on the buy side of the market by large speculative traders.

The synchronic relationship could be described as the very definition of cause and effect, and charts like the one you see here appear regularly in the most sophisticated gold market studies published by Wall Street investment houses and such organizations as the World Gold Council and Gold Fields Mineral Services. This graph, however, is like looking at a snapshot. It tells the essential story, but it doesn't depict motivation. When we begin to understand the motivation of the large speculative interests, we begin to get a clearer picture of future prospects. Pursuing this line of reasoning raises an important question: referring to the chart, what changed in 1999 to bring about this dramatic shift in perception and sentiment? More importantly, is that change in motivation enough to create a whole new psychology in the gold market, or is it just a passing fancy? We have had a clean break with the past, based on six important changes in the way gold is viewed fundamentally by these international market movers:

- General apprehension about worldwide stock and bond markets, particularly the U.S. markets
- The aftermath of the Central Bank Gold Agreement, which fixed and limited the amount of gold available for lease and sale

- The atmosphere of competitive currency devaluations currently dominating the trading relationship among the G-7 nations
- The Trend-to-Zero interest rate phenomenon, which has killed the gold carry-trade (although this could very well turn out to be a short-term consideration)
- Mine company dehedging practices
- The long-term trend change to a bearish psychology on the dollar (based on radical growth in the trade and budget deficits)

These factors provide a strong undercurrent for the rapidly growing international demand for physical gold. Subsequently, that growth has spawned a new market psychology in three important arenas in the gold market: the professional trading desk, the hedge fund, and big private money. This has made all the difference on the charts. This shift in sentiment is one of the primary reasons the country entered into a new secular gold bull market in late 1999, and although we will experience some bumps along the way (as these same speculative interests take short-term profits), the primary long-term trend is now appears to be definitively to the upside.

To this analysis let me add a qualifier. The past is not necessarily prologue when it comes to speculative trading. The foregoing analysis is meant as a view for the long-term with respect to owning physical metal. It is not meant to be applied to short-term speculative trading. For that, we would recommend the assistance of a qualified expert in the field of futures and options.

16

P is for...

Pre-1933 European and U.S. Gold Coins: A Versatile Investment Opportunity and Confiscation Hedge

with George R. Cooper, JD

Historic pre-1933 gold coins offer a rich vein of opportunity for the individual interested in combining gold ownership with numismatic investment potential and protection against a possible gold confiscation. These gold coins were minted by various European governments, as well as the United States, during the nineteenth and early twentieth centuries for commercial circulation within those countries. There were hundreds of different mintings in various weights and currency denominations. They were used both in everyday purchases and as settlement between nation-states for trade purposes. As such, they are the surviving remnants of an era when the world monetary system was based on gold money issued at a standardized weight and purity. All British sovereigns, for example, were minted with a pure gold weight of 0.2354 ounces. All U.S. $20 gold pieces were minted with a pure gold weight of 0.9675 ounces. It is because of that standardized weight and purity that these items traded readily back then and continue to trade readily even today. In this section, you will learn why the addition of pre-1933 gold coins has become so important to a large grouping of gold investors; first, as items which track the gold price; second, as collectors' items with medium- to long-term profit potential; and third, as a defense against government confiscation and/or other forms of government intervention in the marketplace.

What is Government Confiscation?

In most nations of the world, including the United States, gold ownership is considered a privilege, not a right. Historically, nation-states have moved against gold ownership whenever economic conditions are such that public flight from the currency or banking system becomes a tangible threat. The most conspicuous and often-cited example of such a flight occurred in 1933 when the threat of bank failures in the United States caused millions of Americans to withdraw their funds in the form of gold coins. The newly elected president, Franklin Delano Roosevelt, reacted to the panic by issuing executive orders that closed the banks and confiscated the gold. These measures were designed to keep citizens' savings in the banks, whether or not the owners believed the banks to be sound and their savings safe.

To understand how conditions might be such that a gold confiscation could occur again, 70 years after the last one, all one need do is attempt to postulate how the massive federal debt (over $7 trillion and growing) and the outstanding international dollar float (resulting from massive U.S. trade and budget deficits) might be reconciled. In previous chapters, we examined how the U.S. dollar enjoys special status around the world as the primary reserve currency. This encourages—some would say, forces—central banks and individual investors globally to hold it.

Bypassing the various circumstances and potential scenarios discussed earlier, let's go right to the heart of the matter: What would be the outcome if the props were kicked out from under this built-in dollar market, for whatever reason, and even a portion of the foreign-held Greenbacks were repatriated to the United States or set loose on world currency markets? Even more importantly, how would the government react to an economic emergency in which individuals, beset either by a devastating domestic inflation or by a deflationary nightmare or both, were fleeing the banks and equity markets for gold as a means of preserving their personal capital? Beyond that, what would happen if our foreign creditors decided that the national debt should now be backed by something other than the government's promise to pay, and forced the United States to bring its gold reserves into play? Although we cannot know with certainty how the U.S. government would react to such a situation, history, even twentieth-century U.S. history, shows us that confiscation has all too often been the option taken by governments threatened with an economic breakdown. Just as gold is the asset of last resort for the individual portfolio, to do service in the most financially threatening times, so it is all too often the asset of last resort for troubled governments. As recently as 1997 during the Asian Contagion, both South Korea and Thailand implemented "voluntary" gold call-ins. The temptation presented by its citizens' gold holdings was simply too facile to resist.

Although not a foolproof remedy (any protection can be overturned by a government trying to save an economy turned upside down), pre-1933 gold coins offer the best protection against a potential government gold confiscation because of their recognized status as collectors' items. That status is based on past legal precedent beginning in 1933, when President Roosevelt issued a series of Executive Orders closing the banks, confiscating private gold, and instituting a long list of other economic controls. All safety deposit boxes were sealed and could not be opened except in the presence of an IRS agent. Penalty for noncompliance was 10 years in prison and a $10,000 fine, which in today's dollars would be closer to $200,000.

Another Executive Order issued eight months later exempted "gold coins having a recognized special value to collectors of rare and unusual coins" from the confiscation. That classification as collectors' items was reinforced in Treasury regulations issued in 1954 stating that all pre-1933 gold coins would be classified as collectors' items, and again in 1962 allowing the importation of all pre-1933 gold coins as collectors' items.

Author Donald Hoppe offers an excellent layman's legal history of pre-1933 gold coins in his book, *Investing in Gold Coins* (1970):

> In 1954, the Treasury Department recognized at last that the time had come to legitimize the numismatic gold market. Consequently, an amendment was made to the Gold regulations, to the effect that all gold coins minted prior to 1933 would subsequently be presumed to be rare and of recognized special value to collectors, without the necessity of further specific determinations by the Treasury.

Among the legalized coins were the fractional (that is, fraction of an ounce) European gold coins such as the British sovereign, German 20 mark, Swiss 20 franc, French angel, and Dutch guilder, to name a few. All are still available today at favorable premiums over their gold content. The popular U.S. $20 gold pieces were also exempted. Few people are aware that, although gold was illegal in the United States, these items traded freely during the period the confiscation was implemented in 1933, and up until gold's re-legalization in 1975.

Whether or not pre-1933 gold coins would escape any future (potential) gold confiscation or capital controls cannot be predicted. Given the weight of legal precedent, this is the best option available for those with these concerns. Ultimately, you, the gold owner, will have to weigh the potential for a gold confiscation and whether or not pre-1933 gold coins should be part of (or the totality of) your gold holdings. This chapter is meant to be an introduction to a complex and controversial subject, and not a definitive study. For that we can refer to a memorandum written by George R. Cooper, gold advocate and attorney at law, and myself, titled "How

Figure 22. **Pre-1933 Coins**

United States of America

$20 Gold Piece
Liberty Design
Gross Weight: 33.346 grams
Fineness: .900 or 21.6 karats
Diameter: 34 mm
Fine Gold Content: .9675 ounce

United States of America

$20 Gold Piece
St. Gaudens Design
Gross Weight: 33.346 grams
Fineness: .900 or 21.6 karats
Diameter: 34 mm
Fine Gold Content: .9675 ounce

P is for...

France

20 Francs
Rooster
Gross Weight: .207 ounce
Fineness: .900 or 21.6 karats
Diameter: 20 mm
Fine Gold Content: .1867 ounce

Switzerland

20 Francs
Gross Weight: .210 ounce
Fineness: .900 or 21.6 karats
Diameter: 20 mm
Fine Gold Content: .1867 ounce

Great Britain

Sovereign
Gross Weight: .2567 ounce
Fineness: .916
Diameter: 22 mm
Fine Gold Content: .2354 ounce

France

Napoleon
20 Francs
Gross Weight: .207 ounce
Fineness: .900 or 21.6 karats
Diameter: 21 mm
Fine Gold Content: .1867 ounce

P is for…

Netherlands

10 Guilder
Gross Weight: .2163 ounce
Fineness: .900 or 21.6 karats
Diameter: 22 mm
Fine Gold Content: .1947 ounce

Germany

20 Mark
Gross Weight: .2560 ounce
Fineness: .900 or 21.6 karats
Diameter: 22.5 mm
Fine Gold Content: .2304 ounce

You Can Survive a Potential Gold Confiscation." The most important point Cooper makes is that this additional layer of protection can be added to your portfolio at a manageable premium over gold bullion coins, and at a cost similar to what you would pay for similarly sized contemporary bullion coins.

Currency expert and gold analyst, the late Dr. Franz Pick once said:

> I am afraid that one day the government will indeed call gold in. Gold bullion will be subject to confiscation. This is one big advantage to numismatic gold, such as the double eagles. It is an idiosyncrasy of governments that although they may prohibit ownership of gold in any form, they are reluctant to touch collections of numismatic gold coins. Today, there are some 49 countries that forbid ownership of gold by their citizens, but do allow holding gold coins for numismatic purposes. Even Soviet Union and Eastern European countries legally tolerated] the acquisition of numismatic gold coins. So these are the only gold holdings that could be kept in your safe deposit box without any fear of confiscation.

Historically, collector gold coins have been treated differently under U.S. law than bullion, and that treatment generally has been favorable. Since a confiscation would likely come without warning, purchasing pre-1933 European and U.S. gold coins is something to be approached at the outset, and not left on the back burner until the unthinkable happens.

Investment Potential

Another consideration with respect to pre-1933 gold coins, particularly the European variety, is the latent investment potential they represent numismatically. This potential is not too different from the one presented by U.S. $20 gold pieces and silver dollars in the 1950s and 1960s. This was when early accumulators were able to acquire quality specimens in bulk at slight premiums over the bullion price, then put their acquisitions away and wait for the market to come to them. Those investors experienced multiple returns later (during the gold bull market in the 1970s and 1980s), when scarcity and quality began to influence pricing. Bags of uncirculated silver dollars and rolls of $20 gold pieces then became eligible for culling and selling at premium prices by grade, date, and mint mark.

There is no way of knowing with certainty whether or not a similar situation will develop with pre-1933 European gold coins in the near future, but the opportunity presents little or no additional risk for those who already have an interest in owning gold. Historic European gold coins offer great, largely untouched, and potentially lucrative opportunities in the field of gold investing today.

No treatise on the subject of pre-1933 gold coins, even a sketchy one such as this, would be complete without a mention of one of my favorite gold investments—the United States $20 gold pieces in low-grade uncirculated condition. If gold is the immovable North Star of investments—the center around which the universe of financial assets rotates—then pre-1933 $20 gold pieces are the solid foundation upon which the modern gold portfolio is constructed. Pre-1933 $20 gold pieces, which contain nearly an ounce of gold (0.9675 ounce) loosely track the gold price. These, too, are considered collectors' items by the government in many of the laws and regulations concerning gold promulgated since the early 1930s. The Liberty, minted from 1840 to 1907, and St. Gaudens, minted from 1907 to 1933, have become the most frequently traded because their prices are usually close to the bullion value, yet they are still viewed as collectors' items. In the seminumismatic grades, their value is greatly influenced by the gold price. The premium expands or contracts due to strengthening or diminishing demand. This range can vary widely, presenting trading opportunities of which many have taken advantage over the years.

Unlike the pre-1933 European gold coins, which trade essentially in two grades, circulated and uncirculated, U.S. $20 gold pieces are offered in a range of grades, including several uncirculated grades. *Grade* refers to the state of preservation, or quality, of a coin. A rule of thumb: The higher the grade, the greater the spread between the intrinsic gold value and the purchase price. The lowest uncirculated grades are the best for individuals looking primarily for a gold investment. As you ascend the grading scale (which starts at mint state 60, the lowest uncirculated grade and move incrementally toward mint state 70, a perfect coin (and virtually unattainable in old coins), the price goes up and the separation between gold value and numismatic value becomes more pronounced. If you purchase gold coins in the mint state 62 or higher, it is essential to have them graded and authenticated by one of the nationally accepted grading services: the Numismatic Guaranty Corporation (NGC) or the Professional Coin Grading Service (PCGS). Because the grading by these services is widely accepted around the country, you will increase your liquidity and the market for your coins when the time comes to sell. Independent grading is not crucial in purchasing the basic uncirculated coins (mint state 60 or 61) as long as you are purchasing them from a reputable gold firm. In the late 1920s, just prior to the stock market crash, many of America's wealthiest investors purchased $20 gold pieces and shipped them to Europe for storage. A huge hoard has existed there ever since. As a result, most of the $20 gold pieces purchased by today's investors are making their way back to the United States from Europe.

The question is often asked whether the supply of historic gold coins, both American and European, is likely to hold up. Some say the supply is good and should last a long time. Others say the supply is dwindling, and it would be in your interest to accumulate as many as you can, as quickly as you can. It is a matter of common sense, given the limited supply and burgeoning demand discussed earlier in this chapter, that the supply will run out some day. The best course of action is to accumulate in a steady fashion until you have reached your portfolio goal, then sit back and see what happens. Owning gold is important. Owning the right kind of gold is crucial.

17

Q is for...

Quotable Notables on the Subject of Gold

Thousands of words have been written over the centuries about gold—some flattering, some not. Although the world has changed considerably since gold was first used as money in ancient times, the varied human reactions to gold haven't changed at all over the centuries. Some have understood and valued gold. Others have seen it as an impediment to their political and economic designs. Some have seen it as a symbol of greed. Others have seen it as a symbol and instrument of freedom. Whatever the case, gold has indeed raised passions as well as a sense of practical security in the human soul, as noted in the following quotes supplied by the World Gold Council:

There are about three hundred economists in the world who are against gold, and they think that gold is a barbarous relic—and they might be right. Unfortunately, there are three billion inhabitants of the world who believe in gold.
—Janos Fekete (1912–)

Q is for...

Regardless of the dollar price involved, one ounce of gold would purchase a quality man's suit at the conclusion of the Revolutionary War, the Civil War, the presidency of Franklin Roosevelt, and today.
—Peter A. Bushre (1927–)

There can be no other criterion, no other standard, than gold. Yes, gold, which never changes, which can be shaped into ingots, bars, coins, which has no nationality and which is eternally and universally accepted as the unalterable fiduciary par excellence.
—Charles de Gaulle (1890-1970)

Water is best, but gold shines like fire blazing in the night, supreme of lordly wealth.
—Pindar (522–443 B.C.)

It is interesting to note that the average earnings of an English worker in 1900 came to half an ounce of gold a week and that in 1979, after two world wars, a world slump, and a world inflation, the British worker has average earnings of half an ounce of gold a week.
—William Rees Mogg (1919–)

By common consent of the nations, gold and silver are the only true measure of value. They are the necessary regulators of trade. I have myself no more doubt that these metals were prepared by the Almighty for this very purpose, than I have that iron and coal were prepared for the purposes in which they are being used.
—Helen McCulloch (1808–1895)

Although gold and silver are not by nature money, money is by nature gold and silver.
—Karl Marx (1818–1883)

Like liberty, gold never stays where it is undervalued.
—J.S. Morill (1810–1898)

Gold is not necessary. I have no interest in gold. We'll build a solid state, without an ounce of gold behind it. Anyone who sells above the set prices, let him be marched off to a concentration camp. That's the bastion of money.
　　　　—Adolph Hitler (1889–1945)

The modern mind dislikes gold because it blurts out unpleasant truths.
　　　　—Joseph Schumpeter (1883–1950)

The tongue hath no force when gold speaketh.
　　　　—Guazzo

Even during the period when Rome lost much of her ancient prestige, an Indian traveler observed that trade all over the world was operated with the aid of Roman gold coins which were accepted and admired everywhere.
　　　　—Paul Einzig

As good as gold...
　　　　—Charles Dickens (1812–1870)

You have to choose (as a voter) between trusting to the natural stability of gold and the natural stability and intelligence of the government. And with due respect to these gentlemen, I advise you, as long as the capitalist system lasts, to vote for gold.
　　　　—George Bernard Shaw (1856–1950)

It is extraordinary how many emotional storms one may weather in safety if one is ballasted with ever so little gold.
　　　　—William McFee (1881–1945)

Though wisdom cannot be gotten for gold, still less can it be gotten without it.
　　　　—Samuel Butler (1835–1902)

Gold opens all locks, no lock will hold against the power of gold.
　　　　—George Herbert (1593–1633)

Q is for...

Gold were as good as twenty orators.
> —William Shakespeare (1564–1616)

Gold is a deep-persuading orator.
> —Richard Barnfield (1574–1627)

The balance distinguisheth not between gold and lead.
> —George Herbert (1593–1633)

Gold is a treasure, and he who possesses it does all he wishes to in this world, and succeeds in helping souls into paradise.
> —Christopher Columbus (1451–1506)

In spite of all the romantic poets sing, this gold my dearest is a useful thing.
> —Mary Leapor (1722–1746)

Gold is pale because it has so many thieves plotting against it.
> —Diogenes (412–323 B.C.)

There can be no doubt that the international gold standard, as it evolved in the nineteenth century, provided the growing industrial world with the most efficient system of adjustments for balance of payments which it was ever to have, either by accident or by conscious planning.
> —W.M. Scammell (1920–)

Not all that tempts you wandering eyes / And heedless hearts, is lawful prize / Nor all that glisten, gold.
> —Thomas Gray (1716–1771)

Volumes could be filled with the many words, thoughts, and deeds surrounding gold. And, though times might change, it seems the attitudes of gold's defenders and detractors remain the same.

18

R is for...

Reporting Requirements for Gold:
What You Need to Know

Gains or profits made upon liquidation of an investment must be reported to the Internal Revenue Service (IRS) in the year in which they occur. Most of the time reporting to the IRS is handled automatically by the stock brokerage, bank, or other investment firm. The owner of the investment is then required to file his or her gains on the regular IRS income tax forms. Similarly, the IRS requires that gains investors make from the sale of certain gold bullion and coin items (as listed below) be reported as well.

There has been and continues to be a great deal of confusion about federal reporting requirements with respect to gold purchases and sales. Part of the problem results from the fact that it took the IRS almost seven years to publish regulations on gold reporting from the time they were required by the Tax Equity and Fiscal Responsibility Act. In addition, many gold brokers themselves have an incomplete understanding of the regulations and have often passed along the wrong information to gold investors. It took several years of negotiations between the Industry Council for Tangible Assets (ICTA) and the IRS just to get specific regulations published.

R is for…

Following are reportable items as listed by the Internal Revenue Service. Also shown is the threshold number of ounces that triggers the need to file a report to the IRS. Remember, the reporting requirement occurs when you sell, not when you purchase.

Reportable Transactions

- Gold bars: Any combination 32.15 ounces or more
- South African Krugerrands: 25 ounces or more
- Canadian Maple Leafs: 25 ounces or more
- Mexican Onzas: 25 ounces or more
- Silver bars: 1,000 ounces or more
- Pre-1965 US 90-percent silver coins: $1000 face value or more
- Platinum bars: 25 ounces or more

In addition, more than one selling transaction engaged in for the purpose of circumventing the reporting laws is to be treated as a single transaction. This includes transactions by more than one member of the same family. The report also requires the seller's Social Security number. ICTA warns: "This information is provided to assist you and is not intended to be used by you as the sole guideline for complying with these regulations. You should consult your own tax professional… While a stricter interpretation of the regulations is possible, ICTA believes the above guidelines…fulfill the spirit of the negotiations and the intent of the Internal Revenue Service."

Although gold coins not listed above are now exempt from reporting, there is no guarantee they will be exempt in the future. In fact, since the intent of the law is to raise revenue, it is likely that coins not on the list now will be included in future regulations, especially if the gold price rises. For the same reason, it is also possible that the number of coins required for the reporting threshold will be reduced as the price of gold rises. Remember, from the point of view of the U.S.

Treasury, this is a revenue issue. Finally, even though historic items like the pre-1933 European and U.S. gold coins are exempted from the reporting requirement, that doesn't mean you can escape paying taxes on your gains. You are still responsible for taxes, whether or not the item falls into a reportable category.

In summary, the laws and regulations on gold reporting are lengthy and complicated. If you are in doubt, the best course of action is always to discuss the matter with a tax consultant.

19

S is for...

Storing Your Gold

> *Gold and love affairs are difficult to hide.*
> —Old proverb

You've done your homework. You've met with an experienced gold broker. You've purchased gold coins. Now what do you do with them?

Most investors take possession of their gold and make their own storage arrangements. The following are the some of the most popular options.

Bank Safety Deposit Box

Gold can be stored in a safety deposit box at your bank. This is the option most gold investors exercise. The downside of safety deposit boxes is that items are not insured against theft, fire, flood, or similar disasters. Another potential problem is, if the bank closes during a bank holiday, you may not be able to get to your gold when you most need it. The solution to this problem is to keep some at home and the bulk in the bank safety deposit box. Although this particular storage solution has some drawbacks (as do all the other options), I believe this one to be the safest and most practical for the majority of gold owners.

Personal Safe

Another option is to store your gold at home or at the office in your own safe. Be careful here. I recommend a floor safe because it's easy to hide and difficult to crack. A freestanding safe will also do the job. However, insurance companies usually rate floor safes higher than freestanding safes. If you are thinking about storing gold at home, you might want to consult with a bonded safe company on the various options. You might also consider discussing the matter with your insurance agent before purchasing a safe. Your insurance company might offer coverage on your homeowner's policy. Some will cover gold, others won't.

Midnight Gardening

"Midnight gardening"—burying gold on your property—is another option. There are storage canisters available that do not corrode when buried. When considering midnight gardening, keep in mind the story of the man who purchased a respectable amount of gold and buried it in his backyard. Several years later he sold the house but forgot about his buried gold. He had to make a commando raid in his old backyard in the wee hours of the morning to recover it. There have also been cases of children and widows of the deceased being unable to find buried gold.

In my career as a gold broker, I have had some unusual calls about hidden gold. In one instance, a daughter called to say that she had reviewed several invoices for gold purchased by her now deceased father from my gold firm. Her mother was deceased as well, and before her father's death he had not told his daughter where he had hidden the gold. She hoped her father had disclosed the hiding place to me, and unfortunately he hadn't.

In another instance, a distraught wife, whose husband was not a client of the firm, called to ask if I had any general ideas where somebody might store gold. He had purchased a large amount of gold and hidden it. He had suffered a stroke that paralyzed him and left him unable to speak. He could not tell her where the gold was hidden.

Though fraught with peril, midnight gardening will always remain the chosen option for some gold owners. Approach it with due diligence and care. Always leave instructions that can be easily found by your heirs for where you have hidden gold, or disclose your hiding place to loved ones in case of unforeseen incidents.

Depository Storage Accounts

If none of the options above suit you, the last option is to open an insured depository storage account. Most of the top gold firms can refer a reputable storage facility. The insured storage option is particularly helpful to silver owners who do not wish to deal with the bulk and weight problems it presents. There are two types of storage: Fungible and nonfungible. *Fungible storage* means your gold is pooled with the gold of other depositors. There is no tagging or separation. *Nonfungible storage* means your gold is tagged and segregated. There is no pooling. Most gold owners prefer nonfungible storage because the specific coins or bars they purchased will be sent to them when delivery is requested. With fungible accounts, there are more complicated procedures if you should request delivery, so they are less appealing to investors who know they will someday want their gold in hand. One of the advantages of insured storage is the ability to buy and sell over the phone. These features appeal to individuals who travel and don't want the problems of receiving and storing precious metals.

To avoid market exposure, most dealers will not set a price until they have received your metals in their own storage account or at their offices. The problem with insured storage is obvious. In case of an economic or other emergency, you might have difficulty getting your hands on your own metals for any number of reasons—natural disasters, communications shutdowns, social chaos, and the like.

20

T is for...

Trade Deficits: Signposts to a Long-Term Dollar Decline

Simply put, trade deficits occur when a nation-state exports more than it imports. Some nation-states, like Japan and China, seem to be in perpetual trade surplus. Others, like the United States, seem to be in perpetual trade deficit, as discussed earlier. Whenever a nation-state remains in a deficit position for a prolonged period of time, its currency suffers, the inflation rate rises, and the value of one's savings and investments declines. In the extreme, the decline can accelerate to currency collapse, igniting a firestorm in domestic financial markets; recent examples include Argentina and several Pacific Rim states. Structural trade deficits of the type that exist between the United States and both Japan and China concern many prominent economists, who see them as a stimulus for a major decline in the value of the dollar.

U.S. exports and imports were roughly in balance in 1970. In 1992, the trade deficit ballooned to $36.5 billion annually. By 1995, it had grown to $105 billion. By 2000, it had mushroomed to an incredible $378 billion. In 2003, the trade deficit hit $540 billion—a number that sent a shiver through Wall Street (Figure 23). Few can remember the last time the United States ran a trade surplus; it was 1975. Fewer still can remember a time when we were not beholden to Asia and

Figure 23. **Goods and Service Trade Balance**

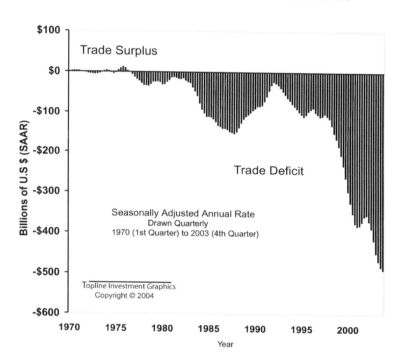

Europe to prop up our bond market by trading their dollar balances for our government debt. The many dislocations in the international economic system brought on by the structural U.S. trade imbalance go beyond the scope of this book. However, we will focus briefly on two of the most obvious: the plunging international value of the dollar and the huge buildup of foreign-held dollar debt.

U.S. Relationship with China and Japan

Nowhere are the dangers to the world economy more implicit than in the United States' economic relationship with the two Asian exporting giants, China and Japan. It is estimated that east Asia holds approximately two-thirds of the world's foreign currency reserves. Japan and China alone hold an estimated $800 billion and $400 billion, respectively, in U.S. dollar reserves, about 17 percent of the total U.S. federal debt.

Recently the *Sydney Morning Herald* openly questioned dollar policy and its potential impact on the Pacific region.

> Around Asian financial circles, there is growing, if still muted, talk of a looming "dollar crisis" equivalent to the sterling crises of the 1960s—when London could no longer support the reserve role of the British pound—unless Washington mends its profligate ways and accepts higher interest rates and taxes. A default by the U.S. government is still unthinkable, but not so a unilateral change in the rules of international finance—akin to Richard Nixon's halt to the convertibility of dollars into gold in 1971, or Franklin D. Roosevelt's devaluation and repudiation of gold-denominated contracts.

Under the circumstances, it is not difficult to understand why Japan and China might be interested in increasing their gold reserves. Even a small shift in the Japanese and/or Chinese reserve position toward gold would have major implications for both gold and the dollar.

Richard Duncan, former International Monetary Fund economist, speaks to what this might mean to the world economy of the future:

> By accident or by design, Japan is carrying out the most audacious endeavour to conjure wealth out of nothing since John Law sold shares in the Mississippi Company in 1720. So far, the results have been impressive. Japan's monetary alchemy has been the most important factor in allowing the U.S. government to finance a $700 billion deterioration in its budget over the past three years without pushing up U.S. interest rates to levels that would pop the wealth-creating property bubble there...

These developments highlight a fundamental question that has been debated repeatedly over centuries: Can governments create money and make the population richer without setting in motion a chain of events that ultimately ends in monetary chaos? We may be about to find out, as Japan tests the hypothesis on an unprecedented and global scale. If this experiment in unorthodox monetary policy succeeds, then we have arrived at a new international monetary paradigm. Governments will have discovered how to finance limitless deficits through the creation of paper money, and we all can look forward to an age of great prosperity. If it fails—as have all past attempts to create wealth from thin air—then the world may not be able to avoid a severe and protracted economic slump as the extraordinary imbalances in the global economy, caused by the explosion of fiat money in recent years, begin to unwind.

In mid-2003, economists at the U.S. Federal Reserve published a paper explaining why the Fed was not "out of bullets" despite having cut short-term interest rates to one percent. That paper stated that "the Fed could even implement what is essentially the classic textbook policy of dropping freshly printed money from a helicopter," if necessary, to stimulate the economy. Today, that helicopter is in the air. But, strangely, it is not the Stars and Stripes that is painted on its side, but rather the Rising Sun. That much is clear. What still is not quite discernible, however, is who is actually in the pilot's seat.

Foreign-Held Dollar Debt

One of the unhappy consequences of the structural trade deficit is that the Greenback is being held hostage by foreign financial interests. Any of these interests can move against the Greenback at any time by simply selling off their bond holdings. Foreign-held dollar debt has become a weapon in the equivalent of an economic Cold War. Just as nuclear weapons were held for most of the twentieth century like a sword of Damocles over the nations of the world, so now are dollar reserves held over the head of U.S. financial markets. To say the least, this puts U.S. stock and bond investors in a precarious position, and makes gold, the stand-alone asset, a critical holding for those who understand the dangers this tenuous synergy implies.

21

U is for...

Using Gold as Money

Since ancient times, gold has served humanity reliably as both a store of value and a medium of exchange. Today, using gold as money seems completely out of place in a world moving toward the elimination of currency and its replacement with credit and debit cards and even cyber-money. Yet the possibility of an economic crash has led many investors to put some gold away specifically for the purpose of buying essentials, if the worst were to happen.

In most instances (even a breakdown), gold owners would sell their gold for the currency in use at the time through the services of a gold exchange, and then use that currency at the store to buy whatever it is they wish to buy. However, some believe that in an economic breakdown with no reliable currency alternative available, citizens will resort to hand-to-hand barter transactions between individuals wherein gold would be used directly as a currency.

Small Gold Bullion Coins

The smaller gold bullion coins (½, ¼, and 1/10 ounce) best serve these purposes. Of that group, the 1/4-ounce coin is the most useful. Most of the countries that mint gold—including the United States, Austria, and Canada—produce coins in the 1/4-ounce size. These are large enough to pass easily as currency from buyer to seller. They can be stacked, stored, and accumulated without the fear of losing a coin or two in the process—something that cannot be said for the smaller 1/10-ounce coin. The premium is slightly higher on the 1/4-ounce coin (over the 1-ounce coin), because the cost of making a coin is roughly the same no matter the size. The more gold in the coin, the smaller the premium per weight because the cost of making the coin is amortized over a larger amount of gold.

Those who foresee a potential for using gold as money and who are concerned with confiscation and privacy matters might consider owning the uncirculated pre-1933 European gold coins as a medium of exchange. These items approximate 1/5 to ¼ ounce of gold. When you purchase goods, there are no reporting requirements on these coins for you or the seller, and they provide an extra degree of safety with respect to potential confiscation.

Using Silver Coins

In addition, you might want to consider a bag or two of silver coins—$1,000 face value, pre-1965 U.S. silver coins. The old standard recommendation of one bag per family member living with you still stands. U.S. silver dollars are still recommended occasionally for this purpose, but the premium is relatively high. The greatest advantage of silver dollars is that they fall under the 1933 dateline with respect to confiscation. Silver rounds and one-ounce silver coins of various manufacture, including the U.S. and Canadian mints, are another alternative, although the premiums are relatively higher.

Having money to barter could be crucial during an economic breakdown. It makes sense to have some gold and silver put away for this purpose. This is not a complicated problem. This advice should suffice in the event of a breakdown.

22

V is for...
Vital Statistics

G old is one of the densest of all the chemical elements. It is the most malleable metal. One ounce of gold can be drawn into a wire about thirty-five miles long. Gold is chemically related to copper and silver. It is highly resistant to chemical change and cannot be dissolved in common acids. Gold does dissolve, however, in aqua regia (a mixture of nitric and hydrochloric acids) and in cyanide.

This chapter is a compilation of vital statistics for all those who have questions about gold's physical and chemical characteristics, but don't know where to get the answers.

Chemical symbol for gold: Au

Atomic number: 79

Atomic weight: 196.967

Specific gravity: 19.32

Tensile strength: 11.9

Melting point: 1,063 degrees

Hardness (Brinell): 25

Occurrence of gold in the earth's crust: 0.005 parts per million

Estimated mine production: 100,000+ tons since gold was first discovered

First gold coin: Minted by Croesus of Lydia about 560 B.C.

Weights & Measures

1 troy ounce = 31.1034 grams

1 troy ounce = 480 grains

1 troy ounce = 20 punts

3.75 troy ounces = 10 tolas (Indian Subcontinent)

6.02 troy ounces = 5 taels (China)

32.15 troy ounces = 1 kilogram

32,150 troy ounces = 1 metric ton (1,000 kilos)

1 troy ounce = 1.0971 ounce avoirdupois (U.S.)

Standard Investment Bar Sizes

400 troy ounces (12.5 kilos)

32.15 troy ounces (1 kilo)

100 troy ounces (3.11 kilos)

10 troy ounces

1 troy ounce

In addition, a wide variety of smaller bars by various manufacturers is not deliverable to any exchange, but trades among makers in smaller markets. Troy weight is based on a pound of 12 ounces and an ounce of 480 grains. It is the universal measure by which gold is weighed and sold in all international markets.

V is for...

Carat Gold Conversions

24-carat = 0.995 to 0.9999 pure (fine) gold

22-carat = 0.916 pure (fine) gold

18-carat = 0.750 pure (fine) gold

14-carat = 0.583 pure (fine) gold

10-carat = 0.4167 pure (fine) gold

Gold jewelry purity is always classified in carats (also *karat*). A carat is the traditional measure of purity contained in the alloy of gold used to make a piece of jewelry; the scale ranges from 1 to 24, with 24-carat representing pure gold. Carat measure is seldom applied to bullion or bullion coin products.

The foregoing is not meant to be a complete compilation of gold vital statistics, but merely an attempt to cover some of the more salient terms and characteristics encountered by gold investors on a regular basis.

23

W is for...

What Should I Do and When Should I Do It? A Sensible Gold Strategy

Investors interested in purchasing gold often ask, "When do you think I should buy my gold?" The short answer is "When you need it." You cannot approach gold the way you approach equity investments. Timing is not really an issue. The real question is whether or not you are diversified and protected against the potential uncertainties ahead—inflation, deflation, hyperinflation, depression, stock market panic, currency collapse, or bank closures. If you do not own gold and you feel you need to, the best time to start is now. It is better to be a day early than an hour late.

That question about when to buy gold, however, infers another question: Do you think the price will go up soon? As a gold broker, up until recently, I have held to the fundamental philosophy outlined in the first edition of this book: For most investors, gold is essentially an insurance and portfolio hedge. However, I now believe we have entered a new era for gold—one separate from anything we've seen in the past two decades and more reminiscent of the 1970s, when huge price spikes in relatively short periods of time produced extraordinary profits.

Figure 24. **Gold Price**

London PM Fix
Daily in US dollars per ounce

Topline Investment Graphics
Copyright © 2004

Because of this, I now believe that gold should no longer be viewed just as a portfolio hedge—although it hasn't lost any of the qualities that make it such—but also as a vehicle for portfolio gains. To me, this amounts to the best of all possible worlds for the gold owner. There is little question that every portfolio needs the hedging, safe-haven characteristics of gold as long-term portfolio insurance. Now I believe that insurance offers extraordinary investment potential based on the possible rapid depreciation of the dollar and its loss of status as the world's only and primary reserve unit.

At the same time, forecasting the price is at best a risky and complicated undertaking. Price swings up and down can be, and probably will be, violent. Already we regularly hear complaints of gold's volatility. The questions become, "How should I approach gold with these circumstances in mind? What would be the most advantageous strategy?"

Implement a Strategy

For most investors, the key to successful gold investing will not come from *predicting the price* on a short-term basis, but from *implementing a strategy* that takes advantage of gold's well-documented and clearly discernible long-term behavior. On the long-term charts, the most telling aspect of this behavior is defined by the spikes (Figure 24). For a variety of economic and political reasons, gold has a tendency to remain flat over extended periods of time, then break to the upside, usually peaking at multiples of its starting point. Without a crystal ball, taking advantage of these spikes on a short-term basis is difficult; however, there is a strategy that makes good sense under the circumstances.

From 1933 to 1971, there was scant private gold ownership in the United States simply because the dollar was backed by the enormous gold reserve in Fort Knox. These were the days when the popular press touted the dollar as being "good as gold." All this changed in 1971 when Richard Nixon severed the link between the dollar and gold and set the Greenback free to fluctuate against the world's other major currencies. Suddenly the gold price began to rise in world markets and ownership became a matter of interest not only for American investors but for investors around the world. These factors ushered in a whole new era for the gold market.

Gold Spikes

During the 1970s, the gold price spiked on two occasions. In 1974, it reached the $200 level—an almost sixfold increase from the $35 benchmark bottom. After retracing to $100 in 1976, it spiked again in early 1980 to $875—almost nine times its interim bottom price. In Figure 24, the average annual gold price is graphed on the logarithmic scale to show the comparable, relative strength of the two spikes, a reality that washes out on a standard, arithmetic chart. The logarithmic chart also emphasizes the range-bound gold price of the 1990s, a circumstance some analysts equated with the $35 to $42 price range that preceded the 1970's bull market. After a descent into the $260 range, gold broke to the upside in 1999 and subsequently made several forays over the $400 mark by early 2004.

Long-Term Strategy

Is the current trading range signaling another, even more pronounced spike to the upside? Chances are that it is, although as pointed out earlier, predicting when the move will begin is difficult. The best strategy for most investors will take advantage of gold's historic price behavior, this tendency to spike. It is difficult for investors to take advantage of these spikes through short-term derivative instruments like futures contracts, options on futures, or bank leverage programs simply because it is so difficult to predict when the spikes will occur. If a leveraged investor were to get lucky and catch a spike, the returns would be phenomenal, but the odds weigh heavily against this happening. Statistics show that 85 percent of all investors in futures and options lose money. That percentage is probably higher with leveraged gold investments.

Instead, the best way to take advantage of gold's price behavior is through a long-term accumulation program of the physical metal itself, following the guidelines in Chapter 10. The strategy is to accumulate regularly and hold through all the minor ups and downs while the primary trend carries the metal higher. In this way, you buy and store for the upcoming spike, taking full advantage of the upside without the risk present in the options and futures markets. Given the well-known nature of gold to spike, this strategy to accumulate and hold is probably the best for the majority of gold owners and makes good sense for covering both the uncertainties and profit potential likely to surface as the twenty-first century unfolds.

24

X is for...

XYZs of Gold Investing: Closing Thoughts

When the international monetary system was linked to gold, the latter managed the interdependence of the currency system, established an anchor for fixed exchange rates and stabilized inflation. When the gold standard broke down, these valuable functions were no longer performed and the world moved into a regime of permanent inflation.
—Robert A. Mundell, Nobel Laureate for Economics, 1999

The case for gold ownership in the modern era rests on two fundamental premises. First, in the absence of a gold standard, there is no discipline on the issue of paper currency. As a result, individuals would be well served to put themselves on the gold standard through private gold ownership as a means to preserve their assets. Second, the sound fundamentals of gold—particularly the wide gap between international usage and mine production—will ultimately push the price upward.

Throughout this book, I have tried to offer the kind of practical advice I would provide any client who asks for it. I have tried to picture myself sitting with a potential gold buyer and answering the typical questions he or she would ask, if

Figure 25. **Gold Standard Versus Fiat Dollar Standard**

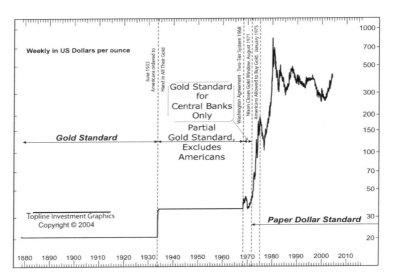

we both had the time to cover the various aspects of gold ownership in great detail. Buyers inevitably want to know what's going to happen with the gold price. I always tell them that if I knew what was going to happen with gold, I would mortgage myself to the hilt and put it all into gold. But I don't know what's going to happen with gold in the short run. Neither does anybody else. We have a good idea what's going to happen over an extended period of time based on historical analysis, the fundamentals, and so on. But in the short run, just about anything can happen. And it usually does.

Markets, if anything, are a humbling experience. Even the best analysts are usually wrong more times than they are right. With gold, the best advice, as I have proffered more than once in this book, is to buy and accumulate over the medium- to long-term. Buy what you feel you need, and then sit back and watch the show.

History has shown that whenever the gold backing for paper money is removed, inflation ensues. This is no less true in the United States than it has been in many other countries throughout modern history, including some of the recent inflation debacles in East Asia and South America. Whenever government management of the currency plays a critical role in its value, that value is eventually undermined, diminished, and finally destroyed. In *The Dollar Crisis: Causes, Consequences and Cures,* former World Bank and International Monetary Fund economist Richard Duncan summed up the gathering storm in financial markets this way: "The economic house of cards built with paper dollars has begun to wobble. Its fall will once again teach the world why gold—not paper—has been the preferred store of value for thousands of years."

The nearby graph (Figure 25) contrasts the gold standard years, 1900 to 1971, to the era of the fiat dollar standard, 1971 to the present. Gold showed remarkable stability when it was the centerpiece of the world's monetary system. As a result, the dollar and inflation were also stable. The dramatic upsurge in the gold price came after the gold backing was removed from the dollar in 1971 and the government was free to conduct monetary and fiscal policy without the discipline of the gold standard. Inflation rates jumped aggressively, and so did gold prices.

It is not overly simplistic to say that the twentieth century was divided into two easily discernible eras: the era of gold-backed money and the era of the fiat dollar. For those who understand those two economic eras, the idea of gold ownership in the present era becomes a completely rational decision based on the lessons of history. From time to time, financial historians and gold market analysts talk about the ongoing war against gold waged by the central banks of the world, particularly by the United States, as part and parcel of this era. Unfortunately, this has not just been a war against gold; inadvertently, it has also been a war against the dollar. It is a war that, over the long run, gold is winning and the dollar is losing.

Few Americans know that in 1945, the U.S. gold reserve amounted to 22,000 tons; at over 50 percent of the world's aboveground stock, this was the largest hoard on earth. Now the U.S. Treasury's gold reserve stands at a little over 8,000 tons, or 8 percent of the world's total. Most of that gold was expended to defend the dollar's role as the centerpiece of the international monetary system during the 1960s and 1970s. At one time, 70 percent of the world's gold reserves were held by governments and their central banks, with the U.S. Treasury holding the single greatest portion. Now, more than 70 percent of the gold is in the hands of private individuals worldwide. Ironically, they hold it as security against the potential breakdown of the dollar-based international financial system it was sold to defend. At the same time, many of the world's central banks, perhaps because they sense danger, are in a dollar reduction mode. The dollar, in the bigger picture, is slowly fading, and gold is once again in ascendancy.

Although all of this bodes well for the gold price in the future, it does not bode well for the United States and the dollar. This nation must get its financial house in order. If it doesn't, the challenges to the dollar and the U.S. economy will continue with potentially even more punitive and unfortunate results. As a financial antidote, a diversification into gold by American investors makes a great deal of sense. This book intends to serve as a means to that end. It embodies the notion that it is a matter of common sense to prepare for the worst and hope for the best. Having traveled this far, you are now prepared to become proactive in adding gold to your investment portfolio. If, in the end, you are able to say that this book opened the door to ownership, then it will have served its purpose well.

Appendix
Historic Gold Prices
London's Gold Bullion Market
Yearly Average Price

Year	Price	Year	Price	Year	Price
1900	18.96	1935	34.84	1970	36.02
1901	18.98	1936	34.87	1971	40.62
1902	18.97	1937	34.79	1972	58.42
1903	18.95	1938	34.85	1973	97.39
1904	18.96	1939	34.42	1974	154.00
1905	18.92	1940	33.85	1975	160.86
1906	18.90	1941	33.85	1976	124.74
1907	18.94	1942	33.85	1977	147.84
1908	18.95	1943	33.85	1978	193.40
1909	18.96	1944	33.85	1979	306.00
1910	18.92	1945	34.71	1980	615.00
1911	18.92	1946	34.71	1981	460.00
1912	18.93	1947	34.71	1982	376.00
1913	18.92	1948	34.71	1983	424.00
1914	18.99	1949	31.69	1984	361.00
1915	18.99	1950	34.72	1985	317.00
1916	18.99	1951	34.72	1986	368.00
1917	18.99	1952	34.60	1987	447.00
1918	18.99	1953	34.84	1988	437.00
1919	19.95	1954	35.04	1989	381.44
1920	20.68	1955	35.03	1990	383.51
1921	20.58	1956	34.99	1991	362.11
1922	20.66	1957	34.95	1992	343.82
1923	21.32	1958	35.10	1993	359.77
1924	20.69	1959	35.10	1994	384.00
1925	20.64	1960	35.27	1995	384.17
1926	20.63	1961	35.25	1996	387.73
1927	20.64	1962	35.23	1997	331.29
1928	20.66	1963	35.09	1998	294.09
1929	20.63	1964	35.10	1999	278.57
1930	20.65	1965	35.12	2000	279.11
1931	17.06	1966	35.13	2001	271.04
1932	20.69	1967	34.95	2002	309.68
1933	26.33	1968	39.31	2003	363.32
1934	34.69	1969	41.28		

Bibliography

To distill over 30 years of study in the fields of economics, economic philosophy, political science, history, and social theory—not to speak of probably hundreds of tracts and analyses on gold and its role in modern society—is a difficult undertaking. The following books, monographs and articles played a direct role in this book. I have also included some of the subscription-based newsletters that have had a profound influence on my own thinking and education over an extended period of time. All of these contributed directly or indirectly to the underlying theme of this book and deserve recognition.

Caldwell, Taylor. *Great Lion of God.* New York: Ballantine Books, 1970.

Cooper, George, with Michael Kosares. *How You Can Survive a Potential Gold Confiscation.* Denver, Colorado: USAGOLD-Centennial Precious Metals, 2000.

Duncan, Timothy. *The Dollar Crisis: Causes, Consequences and Cures.* New York: John Wiley & Sons, 2003.

Gold Avenue. *Gold Encyclopedia & Diary.* London: 2004.

Gold Fields Mineral Services. *2003 Annual Gold Survey.* London: 2003.

Bibliography

Grant, James. *Grant's Interest Rate Observer* (newsletter). New York.

Green, Timothy. *The Gold Companion.* City: Rosendale Press, 1991.

Green, Timothy. *The New World of Gold.* New York: Walker and Company, 1984.

Greenspan, Alan. *Gold and Economic Freedom.* New York: 1967.

Grun, Bernard. *The Timetables of History: A Horizontal Linkage of People and Events.* New York: Simon and Schuster, 1991.

Hathaway, John. *The Folly of Hedging.* City: Tocqueville Asset Management, LP, 2000.

Jastrum, Roy. *The Golden Constant.* New York: John Wiley & Sons, 1977.

Jenkins, G.K. *Ancient Greek Coins.* New York: G.P. Putnam & Sons, 1972.

Kindleberger, Charles. *Manias, Panics and Crashes: A History of Financial Crises.* New York: John Wiley & Sons, 1978.

McGeveran, William A., Jr. (Editor). *The World Almanac and Book of Facts 2004.* New York: World Almanac Books, 2004.

Nichols, Jeffery. *How to Profit from the Coming Boom in Gold.* New York: McGraw-Hill, Inc. 1992.

Rankin, Robert. *The Impact of Hedge Funds on Financial Markets: Lessons from the Experience of Australia.* City: Reserve Bank of Australia, 1999.

Russell, Richard. *Dow Theory Letters* (newsletter). La Jolla, California.

Scientific Market Analysis. *The Nightmare German Inflation.* Princeton, New Jersey: 1971.

Teeple, John P. *Timelines of World History.* London: DK Publishing, 2002.

Turk, James. *Freemarket Gold & Money Report* (newsletter). North Conway, New Hampshire.

U.S. Department of Commerce. *Economics and Statistics Administration. The Statistical Abstract of the United States:*

National Data Book. Washington, D.C.: U.S. Government Printing Office, 1995–2003.

U.S. Department of the Treasury. *Treasury Bulletin.* Washington, D.C.; U.S. Government Printing Office, 1996–2003.

U.S. Department of the Treasury, Bureau of the Public Debt. *The Debt to the Penny.* Washington, D.C.: U.S. Government Printing Office, 2004.

World Gold Council. *Gold Demand Trends, A Quarterly Publication.* New York and London: 1996–2003.

World Gold Council. *The Gold Borrowing Market: A Decade of Growth.* Prepared by Ian Cox. Geneva: 1996.

World Gold Council. *The Management of Reserve Assets: Opportunities and Risks in a Multi-Currency System.* Prepared by Dr. H.J. Witteveen. Geneva: 1993.

World Gold Council. *America's Deficit, the Dollar & Gold.* Prepared by Tim Congdon. London: 2002.

Index

coins, 18–25, 89, 90, 110,
147
counterfeiting, 24
dealers, 97
forms of payment, 28
grade, 111, 112, 130
numismatics, 109-113,
123
population, 112, 113
price comparisons, 28
pricing,
shipping, 28
sizes, 150
supply, 57
Bush, George H.W., 10, 65,
70, 75, 76
Bush, George W., 7, 10, 65,
70, 77, 78

C

Caldwell, Taylor, 71
Canada
Maple Leaf, 18, 21, 22,
137
reporting requirements,
137
capital controls, 89
capital gains taxes, 113
carat, 151
carat gold conversions, 151
carry-trade, 47, 119
Carter, Jimmy, 65, 74
CBS MarketWatch, 38
Central Bank Gold
Agreement, 47, 50-52,
118
Signatories, 52
central banks, 31, 42, 47, 97
gold purchases, 56
gold sales, 47
certified deposits, 16, 102
China, 70, 99

economic relationship,
144
entering gold market, 56
choosing gold firm, 25-30
Christmas surprise
see Mexican peso
Cleveland Federal Reserve,
65
Clinton, Bill, 7, 10, 65, 76
CNNMoney, 65
coins
American Eagle, 18, 20,
24
Australian Kangaroo, 18,
21,22
Austrian Philharmonic,
18, 21, 22
bullion, 18–25
Canadian Maple Leaf, 18,
21, 22, 137
collectable, 18
commemorative, 92
dealers, 23
exotic, 92
grade, 111, 112, 130
Great Britain sovereign,
16, 67, 120, 123, 126
French franc, 125, 126
Liberty, 124, 129
Napoleon, 126
Netherlands guilder, 123,
127
numismatics, 109-113
population, 112, 113
pre-1933, 18, 77, 89, 90,
110, 120–131
rare, 26
South African
Krugerrand, 18, 21, 22,
137
St. Gaudens, 124, 129
supply, 57

Index

Index

Index

Index

About the Author

Michael J. Kosares is the founder and president of USAGOLD-Centennial Precious Metals, one of the oldest and most prestigious U.S. gold firms serving private gold investors. *The ABCs of Gold Investing* is considered one of the top introductory treatises on gold investing.

Kosares has been widely interviewed for his views on gold and the economy. He is also the author of numerous articles and booklets on gold investing, and is the editor of the popular gold market newsletter, *News & Views: Forecasts, Commentary & Analysis on the Economy and Precious Metals.* He also comments frequently on the state of the gold market and the economy at his Web site, www.usagold.com, and through his Weekly Client Letter by email.

Kosares may be reached through his Web site or by contacting USAGOLD-Centennial Precious Metals, P.O. Box 460009 Denver, CO 80246. (800) 869-5115.